BI

MW00914794

THE MASK,

BEYOND

THE MIND

DISCOVER WHO YOU REALLY ARE

BY RUDY DANIEL

TABLE OF CONTENTS

INTRO

From the point of view of the regular, worldly phenomena called society, I'm an ordinary person—just another guy. A cool one? Yeah. Funny, and easygoing? Sure. Charming? Mysterious? The root of all evil? I guess so.

I have a different face for every individual that tries to figure me out. When asked about myself, all I can say is: "I am whoever you choose me to be." Because honestly, it's up to you.

The intention of this book may be perceived as unpopular by those people who want to believe in something. I'm here not to create another belief system but rather to make you question yours. My goal is to help you get rid of the nonsense you have unknowingly collected and throw it away. Why? Because when you do, you have a chance to live and celebrate your individuality—not simply to survive.

My story is in a way your story. It's a story you can relate to because I know now that most of us go through very similar paths in life. Although it appears that everyone is so different, when examined closely, we are very similar in many ways. We share the same core experiences in life, and as different as they might be, they are, at their roots, the same.

Some of us tread carefully through life as if there was a way out alive. Some of us take more risks, ask more questions and put ourselves out there, and some of us show up like rock stars and go out like moths to a flame. Who am I in this arrangement? Who knows, but surely I'm not the careful type.

I'm sharing it with you not to push a conventional go-get-it attitude often found in self-help books, but to spark inspiration and curiosity. You won't find calls to wake up early and grind to become your best version— this isn't that kind of book.

Some would see my story as a way to kick off their path to self-realization or liberation, and others would dismiss it. Nevertheless, this book will pop up pivotal questions, and shed light on different planes of reality and points of view that may have passed you by your entire life.

I'm not a scientist or a mystic. You could say that I'm a philosopher that went outside the perimeters of the institution to test out his philosophy in real life, or in other words, I live by what I say. This is my experience, my self-evident interaction with the universe on a daily basis over a lifetime of almost 40 years.

In a way, this book has written itself and can't be attributed to me. It is the representation of the unified field we live in, where ideas and imagination are phenomena of the collective mind, the collective consciousness. So to whom it may concern, I hope it serves you well.

To all those who venture into the mysteries of the universe: Even though reality is veiled by the active search for it, it appears that only the seekers manage to uncover it.

CHAPTER 1:

ORIGINS

I was born in the Soviet Union in the 80s, and grew up at the time that it was collapsing. The whole thing was falling apart, breaking people's lives into pieces, and its devastation was well noticed all across the Soviet empire… the empire that had watched its promises of peace and fulfillment wash away into the abyss of the past. Life back then was not fancy, especially for a middle-class family like mine.

There were times when we had no hot food because of endless electricity shutdowns or having to wear old clothes year after year. Not a nomination for "The best childhood experience ever."

I remember myself as a pretty happy child with an almost borderless imagination. To say the least, I was always intrigued by the immense beauty and strangeness of the world I found myself in, and looking around I saw mystery, magic, possibility, and adventure.

My childhood was full of unexplained phenomena and mystical experiences. But at the time, there was no one around to point it out as a "Real" experience. Instead, all I got was, "Oh, just forget it, it's your imagination." And who could say what imagination really is, especially to a child? Is it valid? What determines what is real and what is not? I didn't understand any of this.

My first mystical experience occurred when I was six years old. Writing these words now, I can still remember the visuals, feelings, and details, like they never really went away.

One night, in our three-room apartment, I lay in bed and fell asleep. While I slept, I had a full-blown vivid dream, my first full dream that I recall. In my dream, I was physically about twenty years old. The location was somewhere in Europe: 17th century or so according to the people's clothes and language.

In the dream, two men dressed as soldiers were fighting me over something. I did not understand what the reason for the fight was or why it started in the first place, but it was too late to ask—it was a fight to the death.

I clearly remember how the two soldiers lured me into a space that was narrowing down more and more. The space became smaller and tighter while I was fighting for my life, swinging my sword with skill.

After a long, hard fight, with my back against the wall, it finally happened... I was stabbed in the chest with a rapier.

A rapier is a long and slender blade, which sets it apart from heavier, cutting-oriented swords. You know, like the swords of the three musketeers.

I was dead, but was I really?

When I woke up from the dream I was still feeling the pain in my chest. It was so real—real to the extent that I recalled myself feeling it for a long period of time. To this day I still remember the sensations of death, although in a more nostalgic sense. After all, "I'm still alive," as Pearl Jam sang back in the 90s.

About a month later, I was riding around the block on my new Soviet bicycle that was given to me as a birthday gift. To receive a bicycle back then was a truly amazing gift—by today's standards it's like getting the newest PlayStation or the coolest gadget.

After riding for some time, I stopped to rest and looked around, until a boy suddenly appeared and began talking to me.

While he was talking, the scenery changed; it was like a dream. Colors appeared in different hues, shapes appeared without distinct borders, and the sounds I was hearing, including the boy's voice, were a bit off.

The boy spoke, but I didn't understand a word he was saying. For some reason, I was hypnotized and couldn't move. I didn't feel any fear, only surprise and curiosity at what I was experiencing. At a certain point, the boy pulled out a half-broken sword. It was a rapier—pale blue, rusted… and beautiful.

I heard the boy say something about an exchange: a sword for my new bicycle. Nodding in agreement, I sealed the deal and walked home to tell my parents about it. "Such a great deal," I thought, but that thought didn't age well, they were pretty upset about it. The bicycle was expensive, and the exchange was not very appealing to them as far as I could perceive. They went outside to search around the block for the boy to retrieve the bicycle, but he was nowhere to be found. As a result, I got to keep the sword.

In '92 when the Soviet Union finally collapsed, my family decided to use the opportunity that until that point was just wishful thinking: to leave the country. We left the world I used to know in the hopes of finding a better life, a better future.

Fortunately, we immigrated to a sunny country in the Middle East with great weather, delicious food, and positive vibes.

Slowly but surely, I was getting comfortable with the new location, getting to know new people, and embarking on new adventures.

Although I left the Soviet Union, my mystical experiences stayed with me, as if I packed them by mistake with the rest of my belongings.

More and more strange experiences began to occur, and I had no idea what was happening. Nor were the other people around me aware of what was going on. It was as if these experiences were growing more real than ever. One night while I was in bed, the bed sheets appeared to expand and compress over and over, they appeared to be breathing in a way, in and out, in and out.

At times, my leg or arm would grow larger than the room, to an extent I couldn't comprehend. It was a highly uncomfortable and sometimes even frightening experience. I was aware that this phenomenon only occurred solely to me, as neither my friends nor my family could grasp what I was describing. This fact made the experience all the more peculiar.

My parents thought that I was making it all up in my head, in my imagination. But I wasn't, it was real. These experiences were common whenever I went to sleep, night after night, for years as a child and continued throughout my adolescence.

In my teenage years, it began to fade away, but I still sleep-walked around our apartment at night, talked crazy and sometimes wandered beyond the safe entrance door—concerning my parents.

Just imagine yourself as my parents for a moment, waking up in the middle of the night with your teenage son standing next to you with no motion and looking at you in silence... a haunting image for sure.

These experiences would come and go throughout the years. Sometimes they would stop for months and then come back again. During these periods I would grow accustomed to living without the uncanny experiences, hoping they would not come back to haunt me. Yet when they did, they would hit me all the harder.. One time—time itself seemed to operate much faster for me than it was for other people. I could feel speed in all areas of my life: fast walking, fast talking, fast thinking, and fast learning. I thought I was losing my mind, or getting a new, upgraded mind. I had no idea what was going on.

I recall that we had an exam in class with a given time of forty-five minutes. After ten minutes I was done while everyone else took another twenty to thirty-five minutes to fill in their exam papers. I was puzzled with this new reality. How was it possible for two conditions of time to co-exist simultaneously? Was I hallucinating? Could be… but nevertheless it felt real as real gets. And then, as unexpectedly as it had begun, it suddenly stopped. After a few weeks of undesired superpowers, without any preparation or help, it vanished from existence.

Fifteen years of mind-bending phenomena had stopped. I felt better in a way, although I missed it from time to time. The real world that society dictated slowly snuck into my life, but it left a hole in me, and as I grew older, the hole turned into a great void of no meaning.

CHAPTER 2:

MAN, GET LOST

Twenty years have passed, and I lost all the magic I once found in life. I was wired to the Matrix, hard. Like Neo, I was trapped inside a machine world—a world that did not care about my existence. Constantly trying to get that big thing in life, "The thing is coming! It's almost there!" I thought all this time to just keep on going, sustaining my existence day in, day out.

What was this big thing? Who knows? But we all race towards it from the day we know that it's missing in our lives. We always want something, and most of the time we don't even know what it is. Fame? A great career? A luxury car? What does one know about these things before actually having them? Isn't happiness what we genuinely seek? Do we know for sure that fame could make us happy? Or how does it feel to be a great CEO? Or how it feels to be a devoted family man or woman? These are just assumptions we make, a leap of faith towards the future. These assumptions were the big thing that I was looking for, not knowing how it would play out. But the void in my life kept pushing me to look for that big thing, whatever it might be. I wanted it so bad.

So there I was, on the brink of midlife and the thing never came. What a disappointment, what a rat race. Is this all?

Until that point, I accomplished many things in life that were supposed to be that big thing. I had a nice car, a nice place to live only five minutes walk from the blue sea, a nice family, some success here and there, and overall, a life that looked great from a distance, a life well lived.

Going out into the world every morning, walking on the streets of misconception and confusion—where people wander around like zombies or run around like madmen—brought no hope to understand this void in myself. I looked deeply into people's eyes, and I knew for certain they were aware of nothing about this life beyond its superficial appearance any more than I was.

Some people held their belief in God as their big thing. Some preached it on the streets, but it never really worked for me despite the fact that I studied for four years in a religious school.

But for me, the way of religion presented more problems than it solved. Why would an all-powerful God need any disciples, and why would God be so angry about things we can't control? Why should God seek recognition and worship? Why does God need us in the first place? This kind of God appears to be with some serious self confidence issues seeking validation from us earthly souls to raise his confidence higher by keeping us scared and confused throughout thousands of years.

I read many books and studied the big religions, but they were just ideas, certainly nothing compelling enough to satisfy me. If God was real, for sure he would not take this life so seriously, how boring is that?

An all-powerful God, should have no lack, no borders, and no concepts, otherwise it is not a God but something less than a God. So why create a world where people run around murdering each other in the name of God? For what reason? To go to Heaven? Have you ever been to Heaven? It must be the most boring place in the universe.

How long could you stick around in an evergreen place where everyone sits in a committee of the righteous and sing hallelujah all the time? A place Where you're stuck with certain people for eternity? Even Adam and Eve got tired of that place pretty fast.

So these religious ideas were rather ridiculous once I really thought them through. They were all too human, all too shallow. In fact, Hell sounds like a much more interesting place; a great party where all the artists, poets, and remarkable individuals from all generations reside according to religious convictions. It's not that I believe in Hell; the idea of Hell is as equally ridiculous as the idea of Heaven. However, just to get the point across, I had to play Devil's Advocate.

I started to give up on life as a meaningful or satisfying journey, so I turned the world into a "get as much as you can because it's your last one baby!" kind of thing. A mechanical world, a life that arose by pure chance as the material scientists say. A conscious mind in a world of stupid matter made of atoms. A lucky chance that will be over soon when you die, and from there a black hole, forever.

So it was getting money, getting respect, getting appreciated, going on stage, getting dirty in a mud pool of meaningless things we like to call, "stuff, possessions, rewards," and celebrating it… as much as I could. There was nothing else to do besides that anyway.

I turned to entrepreneurship, extreme motorsports, music, drinking, smoking, and anything that could potentially give me that slight feeling. To hopefully get the "edge" again—to feel alive, to fill the void within myself.

"A life free of risks? That's for the weak. Be brave, be ruthless. Look at reality dead in the eye and say— it's my show." I was battling everything, counting wins in money or respect, and collecting defeats in scars on my body and my soul.

My perception of the world was deterministic, harsh, and cynical. I did not have many friends or meaningful relationships left in my life. And honestly, I did not want any of them; they all seemed dull to me, and I had nothing to offer in return. I felt like a kid who got tired of Disneyland, and that all the goodies that he had once appreciated were forever lost.

I knew many ups and downs at this point, and much of my enthusiasm and motivation was left bloody and battered on the battlefield of the human game.

Stumbling through life, I was done. At least it was so for the child in me that had dreamed big and had had a borderless imagination. A child that had just known without asking how. I was drained and empty like an old lion with his best days behind him, carrying the weight of the world on my shoulders. It was the other side of happiness, no doubt. "Life is a drag," I thought.

A song by Pink Floyd kept playing in my head. It said, "And then one day you find ten years have got behind you. No one told you when to run, you missed the starting gun."

It seemed that life was playing games with me, but not in a fun way. Almost everywhere I turned, I encountered disappointment.

As the clock of life continued ticking, I found myself in a state of stagnation, unable to stumble upon anything novel or hopeful that might offer a chance for a positive transformation or meaning.

CHAPTER 3:

COLORS AND SOUND

Time went by and I started to gain some material success in life, and in some sense I became wiser and more mature. New job offers with high salaries and status were knocking at my door, to my ego's satisfaction, but still, I wasn't satisfied.

Life and I have put away our weapons for a while and decided that continually fighting would be a race to an early grave. The society I despised until then was looking up to me and growing more interested in who I was. But I didn't know the answer to that question, so I played many roles in order to satisfy them and myself.

I tried it all, but it was definitely not me. Even success didn't feel that good; it just made me numb inside. It was like a drug to keep me away from myself, from the big questions that I left behind.

"Who am I?" Whenever I lay down in bed at night, walked down the street, or had a conversation, I asked that again and again. I was simply a mirage of a person, an illusion, what appeared as water in the desert turned out to be sand after all.

The real "me", or the real "I" was on a mission to find out who, or what, "I" really is or what "I" was about. And what is this place we call the universe? What is reality?

My wife, as a true people magnet, kept introducing us to new friends. Some were nice and cool ordinary folks, some risk-avoiding boring folks I couldn't stand, and some were strange and dressed funny. But from time to time, we got some real freaky ones, they were the best! I swear, the funniest moments I remember taking place were hanging out with these people, God bless them.

We used to meet up in our flat in the center of the city where we live. It's just a regular city where the Matrix-machine-like reality wakes people up to slavery in the morning, and when they are done, pushes them to the shopping malls in order to stop them from rebellion. Hook them on the goodies and keep them busy, otherwise, they will have too much time to think about this insanity.

In our ordinary flat, we played social games, drank wine, and smoked some quality weed. Those kinds of activities fueled my curiosity; as some of these people were so off the grid yet managed to stay alive. It was a true miracle!

April came and my wife's birthday was on the horizon. We decided to invite some of those new friends to travel to the far south of the country and accommodate ourselves in an authentic eco-house for three days. With nothing to do but lay back, chill, and have some fun, it was a solid plan.

When the day finally arrived, we packed our stuff and traveled for a few hours to get there. Ahhh … some free time from the Matrix, finally.

"Is this peace? Happiness?" I thought. Certainly, it was not the thing that was supposed to be coming, and yet, it felt good. We arrived safely, made some food, and engaged in conversation and relaxed.

"You want some LSD?" asked Joe and pointed his gaze at me. I paused. Joe was one of those off-the-grid friends. "Wow... now wait a minute here buddy... you mean LSD like for real? What now?"

Like most people, I knew that psychedelics or any kind of drugs outside of weed were bad. They can kill you, or even worse, make you go crazy. I remembered the horror stories about LSD from my adolescent years, people flipping out, thinking they are oranges and trying to peel themselves, or believing they are dolphins and jumping into the ocean... horror stories really.

For readers that are not familiar, LSD is a chemical compound that is extracted from an ergon fungus that grows on certain grains. LSD was discovered in 1938 by a Swiss chemist named Albert Hoffman when, by mistake, lucky Albert had a taste of his own medicine, and experienced unexplained visuals and overall radical perception of the world that could be only described as vivid hallucinations or a mystical experience.

LSD has a powerful effect on human consciousness, and people under the influence of LSD and other potent psychedelics often undergo very profound experiences. Most people tend to say that the psychedelic experience is one of their top three most significant experiences in their lives.

So Joe's offer was no joke; this was some serious stuff to consider, and it came out of the blue.

The only positive thing I knew at the time about LSD was that you could see sounds and taste colors. And to that, I'd subscribe all day. But still, it's a psychedelic drug, from a fairly unknown guy, with—relatively speaking—strangers all around, in an eco-house, in the middle of nowhere. Sounds like the beginning of a low budget horror movie. "I'm too smart for that," my brain said to me.

"No thank you mister drug enthusiast, weed is enough for me," I said with a cool look on my face.

Without thinking too much, Joe took a funny-looking paper stamp with a white background, decorated with wave-shaped thin, black lines. He placed it on his tongue and sat back on the soft, outdoor sofa, looking nonchalant as a cat and minding his own business.

I was so intrigued and watched his behavior as if I was watching an unfolding drama. "Ohh man, I hope he doesn't feel like an orange and tries to peel himself," I thought.

To my surprise, Joe was calm and collected. Maybe it's not as powerful as I imagined it to be? Maybe it's a dud? Disappointed, I switched my attention away from him.

Time was stuck somewhere while I was playing my guitar, enjoying the cool breeze and the company of friends around. After a while, I turned my attention back to Joe again. He was holding a nut in his hand, watching intensely, and was bizarrely amazed by it. "What do you see there?" I asked.

No response.

"Is it alive?" I continued the investigation. Joe mumbled and left the space to be alone, with the nut. Maybe, in order to become a nut you must spend some time alone with a nut? Possibly so. He spent most of the psychedelic twelve-hour trip by himself and didn't want any interactions. I thought that it was better to leave him alone as I had no clue about his condition or what was going through his mind.

The next morning, I asked him about his experience, but his words weren't coherent. I figured that he was just a strange, funny guy that takes drugs:

the usual typecast of a "psychonaut," according to the media of "truth" called the internet.

A guy that lives in other planes of reality and reasoning with him would be the same as trying to figure out why he was amazed by the nut, no go.

Nevertheless, I grew more and more curious at the sight of him observing the nut in such awe. It was like he had seen the Divine Spirit, and the thought of it didn't leave me. Mystery was always enigmatic to me, a thing that can be revealed so rarely. I was a sucker for magic, you might say.

"What do you have to lose here, really?" I thought. And so, I collected myself, reasoned it through and through, and finally said, "Screw it, give me some."

It was late afternoon and I had consumed a tab of LSD. I sat there among the group of friends, waiting for something to happen.

After an hour or so, I noticed that the sky was oddly purple, and a slight wiggly ripple was taking place above in a void as if the void was not really a void, it was moving slightly.

"So, do you feel anything?" someone asked me. I replied, "Yeah, the sky is purple, I guess it's working."

A few minutes passed by, and someone brought me a purple geranium and said, "Hold it."

I held the flower and immediately noticed that it was waving from side to side. Not just shaking, but moving elegantly, beautifully. It was dancing.

"I knew it!" I exclaimed as if I actually did "know it." For what reason did I say what I said? I have no idea. I have never seen flowers dance before in real life, at least not on their own. Something deep inside me said that it was "okay," and I couldn't argue, only accept this fact. Somehow I knew this flower and its dance intimately, but if you were to ask me how, I couldn't answer...

Although it felt very strange, I was satisfied, and filled with joy to see it dance.

Time was ticking in the outside world, and the effects of the LSD grew stronger. The visuals became wigglier, and everything was breathing in and out like the bed sheets in my childhood bedroom, but not in a scary or strange way.

They were breathing naturally. Every stone, fabric, or material that was available to my senses did something unusually beautiful.

The sky was filled with fabric-like strings that designed the structure of the universe. Everything was interconnected, entangled, there was no separation anymore between anything, it was whole, one.

Joe suggested a walk, and I followed like a little child that had no clue of how the adventure would unfold. It was already getting dark outside, and as we walked down the street, a strange feeling started to grow on me. My body was light, my filters of the reality I was akin to were slowly peeling away, and I was open enough to see things as they were: important and valuable.

Although things grew more and more grand and outlandish every minute of the experience, I was still "me." The "me" that was from the first time I could feel, "I am", or recognize myself as myself.

We walked a trail to see the view that Joe had discovered earlier that day and kept it a secret for an important event, an event like this I suppose in retrospect.

The trail took us to a desert path that ended on a cliff with a beautiful view. The scenery unfolded under the vast expanse of stars, revealing mountains adorned with red hills and valleys. It almost seemed like we were walking on the reddish soil of Mars.I looked up to the sky and saw trees of energy growing from the top of the mountains to the vast, interconnected network of stars, feeding each other with light.

Joe asked me what I was experiencing as I must have looked so interested in everything, but I wasn't at all interested and rejected any form of chatter.

The world I was experiencing was far too beautiful and too profound to be described in such a primitive medium of communication as the human language. Let alone, at this stage, I could barely speak, and there was no need for it whatsoever.

As we were walking back to the house, time and space began to change their dynamics and the visual effects swelled, exploding into endless variations. But although I couldn't verbalize what I was experiencing, everything was as clear as it could possibly be.

The initial path we walked to get to the cliff turned into an endless maze with an ever changing appearance of what could be only described as—oh wow…. Looking at the ground on our way back, I saw Greco-Roman architecture, I saw that trees were vibrating in different frequencies, and the streetlights were shining crystals, and then… it all hit me.

I was seeing the world all over again, like a small child, amazed by every detail. Tears of happiness came from my dry eyes that had not shed tears in decades.

The long walk back came to an end, and we arrived back at the house. But for me, it was not the same place anymore.

People sat around outside on the cozy, handmade outdoor sofas, passing some joints and having casual conversations, or so it seemed. Laying back and chilling was the thing to do, for most of them at least. I was in a different dimension, a different reality.

The Bluetooth speaker was vibrating the sounds of Estas Tonne's masterpiece "Internal Flight," and I could see it, touch it, smell it. It was all integrating, becoming one, separating, and becoming one again. Each sound had its own color, had its own rhythm and they were mixing up in a divine way. So beautifully that I was fully immersed, blown away. All I could say was "WOW" again and again and again. An auditory and visual experience one could not grasp in the ordinary state of consciousness.

"Here, hold this." Someone gave me a different flower. It was long, and smelled funny. I couldn't tell what flower it was at the time, but it didn't matter. All that mattered was the flower itself.

I held it in my hand when suddenly, I felt that the flower and I were becoming one. It was connected to me, from the edge of my fingertips to the depths of my DNA. I had never felt this sort of connection to anything before in my life.

My breath grew heavier by the second with a panic-like frequency to it. I was hypnotized by the sensation, by the flower's wild, yet beautiful visuals.

It began dancing and manifesting all sorts of shapes, faces, and colors. The visions were not fuzzy in any way, shape, or form. In fact it was the opposite, as if I suddenly saw reality as sharp and concise as it could possibly be. So rich in content and detailed, but at the same time so out of this world, so alien—it just blew me away.

It must have been late, and I was encouraged to go to sleep. I felt the group was worried about the uncomfortable sight of me breathing like a maniac, as I looked at a flower like it was God almighty and kept saying to it, "Wow".

I lay in bed next to my wife, closed my eyes, and there it was: a whole different dimension of reality.

Ever-changing spaces and colors that have not been seen before by any man, with no body, no mind, no thought. I was immersed in experience.

Suddenly, I heard a voice inside me that said, "Wake up, it is just a dream."

As the voice said those words, I immediately felt like someone had taken off my dreamer glasses and showed me another part of reality, a different reality, more compelling and richer. However the experience was short-lived, and I couldn't remember anything even after getting a vivid picture of it, I could just recall the sensation. But time, space, and memory were not the most important factors of reality at the time. I just knew—without knowing how—that its truth was valid.

I knew at that moment that I had touched something beyond my mundane understanding of reality, and had grasped something far deeper than I could have ever imagined.

The LSD trip began its natural descent and got less intense. But I was still so amazed by its revelation, that I got up and went out, leaving everybody undisturbed in their beds.

I sat on the sofa outside, gazing at the stars, experiencing unity with the universe again like in my childhood, full of gratitude and awe.

Realizations about myself and about life kept pouring down over me like rain, and I had no umbrella to frame them, it was pure, and overwhelming.

Finally, when it was almost dawn, I fell asleep.

Although these words might appear as a description of the real events, they are not.

Why? Because words point to something beyond themselves, and the experience is surely beyond any words that could describe it. For example, the sound— water, will not make your thirst go away, it's just a sound, not real water.

When the self-evident experience breaks the boundaries of intellect, understanding, and reasoning, it becomes obvious beyond explanation. So the idea of telling a story is not to explain it beyond any doubt, but to create an image, a form that one can observe from an individual point of view and derive its essence in an elegant way, this is why storytelling is key in marketing and metaphors are key in philosophy and theology.

CHAPTER 4:

SELF-INQUIRY

The next morning, I was confused. It seemed to me that I was not the same person anymore. Flowers, trees, and birds, all looked magical to me again. I couldn't ignore them any longer or treat them as some "background" as I was used to.

When we got home, I began to look up materials and books to read about LSD and other psychedelics. During this, I stumbled upon philosophers and great thinkers, mystics and spiritual teachers who were all talking about these kinds of experiences from their own points of view.

To say that I was intrigued would be an understatement: I was rather obsessed. "How could people live their lives, not even knowing that their perceptions, thoughts, and experiences are just part of one bigger, underlying reality?" was a recurring thought going through my mind.

It kept on pushing my interest further, and I found myself reading about a hundred books after my first LSD experience in a span of one year. Books about philosophy, theology, arts, and so on. Although the books and materials I read gave me a lot of tools to explain the LSD experience, it was still a shell of reality—a symbol of what I touched that evening on my wife's birthday.

Someone once said, "Words are like birds, watch them fly away."

An amazing fact I found when researching psychedelics is that they are (for the most part) absolutely harmless to the body or mind. In fact, before the war on drugs began and destroyed the reputation of such medicines, there were many studies around the world that stated that such substances— like LSD—can cure depression, anxiety, alcoholism, and post-trauma issues.

In terms of harm and toxicity, these substances are considered safe when used in controlled and moderate doses. For instance, LSD is typically consumed in doses ranging from fifty to one hundred and fifty micrograms, which is relatively small. However, it's important to note that the safety of these substances lies primarily in the context of responsible use and appropriate settings.

While they may not be physically toxic, their powerful psychological effects can lead to unpredictable experiences and potential risks, especially in individuals with underlying mental health conditions.

As my thirst for knowledge grew, I tried many types of psychedelics in search of that "thing" that I was always looking for and the knowledge of who "I" am. Tricky stuff I know, but who is this "I" that asks anyway?

One of the strangest mystical experiences that turned a good friend of mine into a believer in the mental world—took place under the influence of LSD.

I was on a retreat with two good friends, we all consumed a tab of LSD and walked around in silence, trying to explore the essence of the experience and the depth of our souls.

It was very similar to the place we visited on my wife's birthday. This time, the location was a very big, Arabic-style tent that could easily accommodate fifteen people. It had colored mattresses everywhere and carpets all over the floor.

Each of us got our own spot in the tent and we spent our time walking in and out of it. I was never a monk, but for those twelve hours, I sure felt like one. No one said a word except whenever we had tea: "Here is the sugar," and so on. Totally silent... almost holy-like.

Suddenly, a ginger cat walked into the tent. An old cat, with life experience engraved as scar tissue in some parts of his body. The cat knew people well, and as far as I could say, he knew we were high and therefore, there was no danger to him.

"Oh oh," I said out loud. All of my friends knew very well about my unbearable, allergic reaction to cats. I've had it since the age of seven when my cat was run over by a car. My heart broke into pieces, and I've had a violent allergic reaction to cats ever since.

Let me clarify. If a cat was in the house and I walked in, I had a minute to get out or else I would get red and itchy eyes as if they were filled with sand, short in breath, and irritated hives spreading across my entire body, a total nightmare. Even if a cat owner stood next to me, I would get red eyes, that's how violent my allergy was.

So, when the ginger cat appeared and refused to leave, I was worried. None of us could really do anything about it as our bodies were in no condition to run around the big tent and try to scare off the cat that knew we were high. To put it simply, it would not be a successful operation.

"It's not safe for me," I said to my friend Demian who was next to me. Demian knew my condition well because he had a cat at home, which I have visited only once throughout our long friendship, and only for a minute or less.

Knowing that he couldn't do anything about it, Demian said, "Maybe this cat came here to cure your allergy." I looked at the cat and accepted the words of Demian as truth in the same way you accept the truth of someone stating their name when you meet them for the first time—a naive truth. The cat stayed inside the tent throughout the whole trip and left at dawn. I was fine, no allergic reactions. "How could that possibly be? Can LSD cure cat allergies? What is going on here?" I thought.

After a few days, Demian called me and suggested that I come over and see if the allergy had mysteriously gone. So I accepted the offer and came over.

I settled onto the couch, anticipating the allergy to kick in and send me home laughing at my poor attempt to stare it in the face and hold the line. The dreadful minute passed... nothing. Five minutes... nothing again. Half an hour later... and still nothing. Demian and I looked at each other in a way that could only be described as, "WTF?"

I petted the cat, played with it even. The allergy went away like it was never there to begin with.

From that day on, I visited Demian every week. The magic was real, and we knew it, but we had no idea how to explain it.

In a span of a year and a half, I embarked on various psychedelic trips with LSD, Magic Mushrooms, DMT, and MDMA, in order to understand what it was all about and maybe to answer the "I" question.

I had the most profound experiences, including bad trips. But none of that got me closer to what I felt that night on my wife's birthday. Yes, it was visually breathtaking. There were new insights, yet, it was not the same, not the thing that I was looking for.

After a while with no satisfying results from the psychedelic realm, I turned to Eastern philosophy with the idea that they may have found a more subtle way to know their true nature, a way much simpler and straightforward. Ultimately, it is the way of just being present in life and seeing things as they are.

As I went deeper into these teachings, I began to see that there is no need to use psychedelics to observe the profound nature of the world. Psychedelics are a door, an invitation, but they could turn into a revolving door if abused, leading to more confusion.

I saw that the essence of this world becomes apparent through comprehending fundamental truths about existence, such as the inherent polarity, or duality of things and concepts like "up and down." Imagine having a continuous experience of "up" without ever experiencing "down"; the concept of "down" would be nullified as there is no reference to it. This principle extends to other aspects of life, like beauty and ugliness, good and bad, right and wrong and so on. Each of these pairs is interdependent—neither can exist in isolation from the other.

In the same way, an organism cannot exist in isolation from its environment. Imagine yourself as a human organism, living your life. The very essence of your existence relies on various elements from the environment. You need air to breathe, the ground to stand on, and food to sustain you with life energy. It becomes clear that you cannot be detached from the world around you. What you perceive as the external world is, in fact, intricately connected to you, much like how a fruit is an integral feature of a tree. This may seem deceptively simple, but when we consider that "up and down" are merely different aspects of a continuous process rather than distinct entities, it becomes evident that everything outside of you is essentially an extension of yourself.

In the grand tapestry of existence, we often encounter pairs of opposites that seem to stand in stark contrast to one another. Examples such as good and evil, joy and sorrow, birth and death, are fundamental to each other. At first glance, they may appear entirely separate, each with its unique qualities and characteristics. Yet, when we look deeper into the nature of these oppositions, we discover a profound connection that binds them together.

Consider the duality of "yes" and "no." On the surface, they represent affirming and negating responses, seemingly at odds with one another. However, the existence of "yes" is dependent on the existence of "no." Without the possibility of saying "no," the concept of "yes" would lose its meaning. They define each other, forming a dualistic relationship that sustains their existence and significance.

Similarly, the concept of "light" and "dark" reveals a profound truth. Light is often associated with illumination, clarity, and positivity, while darkness is linked to obscurity, mystery, and negativity. But without darkness, light would have no context, and its shiny quality would go unnoticed. Darkness provides the backdrop against which light shines brightly. Just as a painting gains depth through contrast, so do these opposing forces; their parts comprise features of the whole.

As I explored further, I came to realize that these dualities extend beyond simple pairs of concepts. The entire universe is composed of an intricate web of interrelated elements. Every living being, every atom, every event, and even every thought contributes to the grand symphony of life. Each part depends on the whole, and the whole depends on each part. In this vast interconnectedness, separateness dissolves, unveiling the unity between opposites.

It is a simple truth, and it goes back to the Chinese philosophy of the Yin and the Yang, the two that co-exist in the one.

When I came to understand this fundamental principle of life, I started to look at the world from a different perspective, a perspective of appreciation and wonder—at least for the most part. I could be walking down the street and be stunned even by some garbage that was strewn about; I could see the whole life cycle of the garbage, its paradox and duality.

The streets outside were the same, so were the trees, and the flowers. But my view had changed and so my satisfaction grew alongside my love for life.

My world was reforming itself without any noticeable changes in the outside world. In short, nothing changed besides my own point of view, and in that, everything changed.

I kept asking myself, "What do I really want in life? What is it all about?" So many questions. I was overwhelmed, digging deeper, hoping the answer could be found in this sort of intellectual investigation.

In Buddhism, the most compelling truth is that the cause of suffering is rooted in desire.

For example: When I want something very much, a negative side and a positive side are created at once. Hope and disappointment arise as a result of desire. This is the same duality I was discussing earlier: a process rather than two different events.

Consider this scenario: If I don't achieve what I desire, disappointment sets in. On the other hand, if my wishes are fulfilled, I experience satisfaction, albeit temporarily, until a new desire emerges. However, this new attainment can also give rise to the fear of losing it, ultimately leading back to disappointment. Thus, the cycle continues forever.

This pattern reveals a fundamental truth: Nothing in life is permanent. Whether we attain our desires or not, both outcomes lead to distinct manifestations, yet they share a common essence: impermanence. In this realization, we question the rationale behind our desires and wants.

Why should we pursue fleeting desires if they can only provide temporary contentment? When understanding the impermanence of these pursuits, the mind opens up to a new perspective.

We begin to observe the ceaseless flux of life, where pleasure and pain, gain and loss, are intertwined in a delicate dance. This awareness invites us to transcend the constant craving for external achievements and explore a deeper realm of inner contentment.

By shifting our focus from external desires to internal fulfillment, we discover a wellspring of lasting joy and peace. Instead of being perpetually entangled in the pursuit of temporary pleasures, we learn to appreciate the beauty of the present moment, embracing life's impermanent nature with equanimity.

Therefore, what could be considered the most basic state of being for someone who has awakened from the illusion of dual reality? It's happiness. Why happiness specifically? Because it represents the foundational condition we all strive to attain. Beyond the pursuits of wealth, accomplishments, status, and recognition lies the underlying aspiration for a state of happiness.

However, happiness cannot be attained by actively seeking it externally, for its essence resides within oneself.

Imagine if I were to assure you right now that you are utterly secure, that this reality is but a dream, and regardless of your actions or perceived missteps in life, you are completely safe. In light of this assurance, you are free to navigate this existence according to your genuine individuality. Wouldn't you find yourself in a state of happiness?

So then, why do we often find ourselves lacking in happiness? It's because, as the poem says: "I, a stranger and afraid, in a world I never made"— or at least, that's how it feels. Fear, as the opposite of happiness and unity, is the driving force of this sensation. And like happiness, it is within us, so it's on us to be aware of it and work with it.

As the great philosopher Alan Watts has put it so beautifully:

"There are two reasons that you don't know what you want."

Reason 1: You have it.

Reason 2: You don't know yourself.

Having reached this profound realization, I shed the old identity of feeling afraid and detached from this world. Instead, I embraced the truth that I am not merely a separate part of the universe that is being kicked around, but the universe as a whole—a boundless and interconnected entity encompassing everything within it.

However, even in the wake of this revelation, my thoughts continued to swarm around me persistently, like relentless unwelcome guests. They seemed unwilling to grant me a moment of solitude.

On a conceptual level, I had assimilated the insights about impermanence and the transience of desires. These ideas had become familiar words I would share with others and repeat to myself. However, within the depths of every mind, there exists not just one voice, but multiple inner voices, each with its unique perspective.

Among these voices, a particular one persisted, whispering doubt into my consciousness, questioning the validity of my understanding. "Are you merely fabricating these ideas?" it taunted, echoing the dismissive remarks I heard during my childhood days.

Despite my analytical exploration and familiarity with this knowledge, there was a lingering uncertainty. It felt like an untested theory, lacking tangible roots in the real world, or as we call it - wishful thinking. The clash between intellectual and non-intellectual understanding was a constant battle between two mighty armies.

The voice of doubt was a manifestation of my past conditioning, deeply embedded in the soil of my mind. It stemmed from the beliefs and judgments I internalized as a young child, leaving a mark on my perception of reality like a madman, in a never ending conflict.

The conflict created an internal paradox. I yearned for my knowledge to find a secure footing in the real world, beyond mere theory. I craved the experiential confirmation that would dissolve the nagging skepticism.

CHAPTER 5:

EGO DEATH

As I continued to engage in a debate about these important matters, I found myself losing sight of which part of me was originally on my side. The inner dialogue seemed like a confrontation between two versions of myself, leaving me questioning the validity of each voice. It felt like an endless puzzle, trying to determine which perspective I should trust.

Have you ever experienced this disorienting feeling? So much noise and contradiction that the sense of self becomes elusive, and you forget whom to believe within your own head. I found myself in that exact situation: sometimes convinced of one thing, only to lose that certainty and then regain it, only to lose it again in a relentless cycle.

Amidst this internal turmoil, I realized that I needed a break from the ceaseless mental battles. Friends and acquaintances offered various suggestions: retreats, immersing myself in nature, social gatherings, or meditation and other spiritual pursuits.

However, none of these options resonated with me. The mere mention of "meditation" or "spiritual awakening" evoked a feeling of repulsion within me.

I came to observe that many spiritual practices, while initially captivating and insightful, would eventually become traps. They might reveal profound truths that resonate deeply with us, leading to an obsession with the newfound wisdom. We cling to it, extract every drop of meaning, and become fixated on the practice until it ends up as an undesired chore.

The very practices that once brought so much good into one's life could transform into grim responsibilities one must repeat. We might witness this in the lives of so-called "serious" meditators and those who consider themselves "spiritually righteous." Their fear of letting go prevents them from finding relief, even as they suffer through the practice. It becomes evident that adhering rigidly to a method is not ideal, as the nature of existence is ever-changing and there is no reason to cling or hold on to it.

The acceptance of any practice as the ultimate truth creates a subtle yet potent trap. It blinds one to the dynamic and fluid nature of life, inhibiting one's ability to embrace the ever-shifting landscape of reality.

Surely, one can use different practices or methods, as methods are a path, a doorway to where one's going.

When you knock on the door, you don't keep on knocking once it is opened. So in the same way, any method is a trap when you consider the method to be the truth. As the knocking opens a door from time to time, so does the method, but nevertheless, it's not the knocking that you're after.

Thus, I found myself being pulled back into the realm of mundane reality. The allure of spiritual enlightenment seemed distant and elusive as I grappled with the complexities of existence and my own inner world. In this moment of uncertainty and disillusionment, I understood the importance of embracing imperfection, uncertainty, and the transient nature of life. The path to authenticity and understanding lies not in rigid practices, but in the genuine exploration of our own unique experiences and the continual evolution of our individual identities.

"Perhaps the time has come to take my experiment to the next level," I thought. A three-day solitude retreat, without any outside stimuli and beyond the reach of the Matrix.

A few days passed by, and my wife said that she had found the perfect place for me called "The Magic Truck". She booked it from Wednesday to Friday next week—It was on.

I thought about taking LSD, but it didn't feel right. I've seen the LSD world many times, and as beautiful and sometimes scary as it was, there was nothing new to find out, at least for me. I messaged my dealer to inquire about some fresh magic mushrooms that could send me to another dimension (or at least that could scare the crap out of me). And of course, he said he had it, he had "Penis Envy" mushrooms.

Although I knew my way around mushrooms, I had never tried those mushrooms before. And yes, it's an actual mushroom that looks like a penis, sort of.

These mushrooms are usually two to three times more psychedelically potent on average compared to other magic mushrooms, and that meant a wild adventure into the unknown.

My dealer assured me that they were one of the most potent mushrooms he had, and I wouldn't regret it.

"Ohhh man," I thought, "am I really going to do this? Sounded like a lot to deal with." Usually, you will need someone around to feel safe if something goes wrong. It is just a measure of mature responsibility, which I lack, obviously.

Thinking it over, I texted my friend who is a "shroom" expert with a diploma from the high dimension institute, and asked, "How much should I take? Is it safe to do it alone?"

"Do not take it alone," he told me. "You got to have someone with you, don't be reckless."

"Well," I thought, "risk-taking is a part of my persona so why not... What can possibly go wrong?" As one of my tattoos states: fortune favors the brave.

Wednesday arrived sooner than expected, and I quickly packed my bags along with my guitar. Accompanied by my dog Teddy, who was incredibly excited about the trip, I was all set to go. We got in my car and into the wild we went. A three-hour drive to the northern part of the country, where people live differently than I do, where everything is greener and more peaceful.

The songs of Eddie Vader that were composed for the movie *Into the Wild* played loudly in the car, and a sense of freedom captured my imagination.

Driving into the unknown adventure, I felt a sense of joy, of not having any specific plan or checklist that needed my attention for the next few days.

As Eddie sings:

"Out here, realigned, a planet out of sight. Nature drunk and high."

Teddy was chilling in the backseat and waiting for the world to change. For him, every adventure was the ultimate one. I was striving to attain his point of view in life as he was truly a great teacher.

He never gets angry, always has fun, and when the time comes, he is able to let go of any good or bad that comes his way. He is a guru, except for the nasty habit of licking his nuts in public, but who is the real guru if not the crazy one?

We arrived early at noon at the Magic Truck's location. It was a long and wide forest with trees stretching in every direction. The magic truck, which had a blue cabin and was carrying a small house, revealed itself to us in the middle of the forest. It was a house on a truck.... How cool is that?

To my surprise, the cabin of the truck was open, and I could actually sit inside and play truck driver. Was it dumb? Maybe so, especially for a middle aged man, but games are forever valid, at any age, even if kept hidden from the judging eye of society.

After thoroughly examining the truck's cabin, I went to check the rest of the place. Outside it had sofas, a small kitchen, an outdoor shower, swinging chairs, handmade furniture, many kinds of flowers, cacti and a fire pit. The overall feeling was that I entered a portal to the soul of the host.

It was me, Teddy, the forest, and the truck. Inside the house there was more handmade furniture, paintings from wall to wall, more cacti and flowers. It had a kitchen, bedroom, and a beautiful wooden shower, too. It was perfect.

While Teddy was running around the forest, cementing his legacy with his own pee, I unpacked, cooked a light lunch, and listened to some relaxing lo-fi beats.

Observing the hands of the watch on the wall, time appeared as floating from the present moment and straight into the past; the diary of the day. But it was for registration purposes only, it didn't mean anything to me at that point.

I was just hanging around, reading a book about Dogen—a great Japanese Zen master from the 13th century that to this day is known to be one of the most influential masters of Zen Buddhism.

And although it was quite gripping, my thoughts began to wander towards the Penis Envy mushrooms I brought with me.

It was an hour or two before sunset and I decided that it was the perfect time to consume the mushrooms because then I would get to see the beautiful forest in sunlight and softly embark into the darkness with a sky full of stars, and rest in the beauty of the universe on the sofas outside.

I stood in the kitchen and began to prepare mushroom tea, to which I will refer to as - the Tea of the Gods. The Tea of the Gods ingredients are as follows:

dried roses, black tea, lemon, sugar, and about four grams of Penis Envy mushrooms. I let the tea cool down for about twenty minutes.

While grappling with myself, I asked, "What do I really want to know?" Well, I guess that it's me I want to know more than anything—my true nature.

It's a mysterious question that is often neglected by Western society, and I was keen to dig even deeper into my very core to find out.

After twenty minutes, the Tea of the Gods was ready to be consumed. I blessed the tea in an elegant ceremonial way and drank it.

After approximately nine, mind-bending hours the trip was over.

In a similar way to my first LSD trip on my wife's birthday, this experience had shaken my very core and everything I knew about myself. It had beautiful, profound moments where the reality of everything was the most simple thing to grasp, and some of it was the most horrific, scary, and insane moments I have ever experienced in my life. This experience many refer to as "ego death."

As terrifying as it sounds, I was willing to take this plunge, to metaphorically face death itself, in pursuit of profound understanding. And so, as that fateful night unfolded, I found myself confronting the darkest corners of my psyche. So dark that even Freddy Krueger would have been crying like a little girl asking for his mommy.

They say that "ego death" marks the demise of the false self, the imaginary person we have so obviously believed ourselves to be. But for me, it wasn't a gentle passing; it was a painful, agonizing death. I felt lost and detached from reality, like a frightened child facing an overwhelming nightmare with no place to hide, and no one around to help. Until one moment, in the midst of this chaos, a revelation struck me like lightning.

I asked myself, "How can I be in pain, or be afraid? I am merely in a room, here and now, and that is the only reality." It was an epiphany that shattered the illusion my mind had woven. Suddenly, I could see through the tricks it played, and the bad trip lost its grip on me.

Amazed by this newfound understanding, I learned to differentiate between my mind and myself. No longer enslaved by the ego's desires, I have discovered that the mind could be a powerful ally instead of a tyrannical master.

As you set foot on your own path of self-exploration, brace yourself to confront your deepest fears and challenge the illusions that obscure your true essence. The ego death is an alchemical process that can potentially lead to the awakening of your genuine self before it is qualified by any experience: the self beyond the limitations of the mind and the illusions of the ego.

Be it a psychedelic trip, a profound mystical experience through meditation or any other way it may accrue, don't shy away from the darkness; it is within the unknown that you'll discover the radiant truth of your existence. Embrace the terror and beauty that come hand in hand, for within the shadows of ego death lies the brilliance of your authentic being.

CHAPTER 6:

IT'S A NEW DAWN

The physical stress that my body experienced during the mushroom trip had drained all my powers. The sunlight slowly brought me back from deep sleep. No dreams this time around, not even a trace. I felt like a passenger returning from a black hole, feeling that I had been there, but had retained no memory of it.

The vivid experience of last night left me speechless, thoughtless, and I was walking around the truck house, observing everything and being in the moment.

I made breakfast with not much desire, but I had to eat. I took Teddy out for a walk in the forest, and it seemed that he was enjoying this time off with me.

The forest was at ease, with little wind. The sun was not too hot either; it was perfect. Teddy, as usual, was busy competing with other dogs for territory and glory.

I watched him with a loving heart, like a father watching his son grow. It was lovely.

A week before arriving at the Magic Truck I was at the bookstore shopping for a gift. A close friend's birthday was nearing, and I wanted to give her a book of great insights. I wanted to give her a different point of view of life, so what could be better than a book?

I searched the bookstore and found Eckhart Tolle's The Power of Now. "I'll take this one," I said to the book lady. "Well, you might want to take this one as well for yourself if you are interested in these kinds of things," she pointed her finger to the book of Don Miguel Ruiz: *The Four Agreements*.

The book was already a part of my library at home, so I refused. Although I had read it a long time ago and I couldn't recollect much of it.

The next day, I was with friends, drinking coffee, when suddenly a conversation about Ruiz's book began. "Strange… I encountered Ruiz's book yesterday. What are the odds?" I thought.

When I arrived at the Magic Truck, I found this exact book resting next to the bed.

I felt as if destiny was calling me to read the book again, and why not? I prepared some coffee, went outside, and lay on the sofa to read. The weather was great, Teddy was chilling, and I immersed myself in Don Miguel's teachings.

Although I had read it before, it came to me in fresh, new, and exciting ways. Don Miguel was playing the strings of my soul with every word, being so far away, but so close at the same time.

From time to time, I felt that I was not reading a book but as if Don Miguel, the Shaman himself, was present, telling me these teachings from within me. I was enjoying the book so much that it took about two hours to read from beginning to end.

I placed the book back on the shelf and wished luck to the next reader, whoever they might be. It is truly a beautiful book.

Time was ticking away while Teddy and I were chilling outside. The trees played their own music with a little help from the wind and birds. Their songs could be heard at various points in the forest, creating melodies that could be understood only at certain moments.

The forest was generous in its abundance and wood was to be found everywhere, and so we went to get some wood for the fire pit.

After a while, we had gathered all the wood we needed, and Teddy grew excited. He was accustomed to fire pits and relished the warmth, accompanied by the soothing music often played during such moments, some say that he is one of the happiest dogs alive.

I lit the fire, made a cup of tea, and began to play my guitar. Usually, I enjoy playing when I'm alone. It takes all the expectations off, with no one around to impress, I am free to make mistakes, take "musical chances," and express myself totally and freely.

I have been playing the guitar from a young age. I just love music. There is something true about it for reasons that need no explanation.

I could go ahead and describe a musical piece like Beethoven's "moonlight sonata" but it will only be a pale description compared to the experience of listening to it, and this is why it is beyond description.

In fact, music is so important because it has absolutely no meaning. One could ask - what is the meaning of music anyway? And there would be no one with an answer that is supported by empirical evidence, it is just what it is, and this is the reason we love it so much. In some cases, music has meaning and mostly it's very poor music, like music that is made to make money, this music emphasizes repetitive patterns and capitalize on trends and fashion in order to increase sales.

Three hours passed by, and I was still going, playing and singing all the songs that were hard-wired inside the repository of my memory. Rock, blues, jazz, soul, country, and even a Mozart piece that I knew by heart.

With smoky, burning wood in front of me, sitting on the soft bench with the guitar in my hands, time had stopped.

Absorbed in the moment, in the here and now, it spoke to me, gently, from within my heart-mind. It was a voice that I could recognize immediately, a voice that has spoken to me before at various moments in my life. It had no sound. It was simply pure knowledge that came instantly, without notice and without inquiry. It spoke straight into my center of knowing.

In Hindu traditions it is said: "Those who know the Brahman(The Godhead) know him not. Those who do not know the Brahman(The Godhead) truly know him." And so it felt, knowing without knowing and understanding without reasoning.

Although it might seem peculiar initially, this experience occurs regularly, much like the way music does. The awareness of knowing oneself or simply being alive doesn't necessitate an explanation; it aligns naturally with the fundamental reality of the experience itself. And so, in a similar manner, I simply knew.

Indeed, the inner knowledge we possess often transcends mere intellectual understanding. Artists, poets, scientists, and musicians have experienced moments of profound discovery without any conscious effort, as if the answer revealed itself naturally. It's a form of meditation that occurs without actively practicing or exerting willpower—an innate state of revelation.

Have you ever found yourself in such a situation? Perhaps, while just sitting quietly without any thought, or walking down the street without particular focus, when you suddenly experienced an epiphany: a clear answer to a question or a brilliant idea that had previously eluded you. It was as if a veil lifted, and you exclaimed, "Why didn't I see this before? Now it's crystal clear!"

Such revelations can occur in dreams as well, where upon waking, we are gifted with life-changing ideas or insights to improve our lives.

Similarly, I had my moment in front of the burning wood, its smoke, and the timeless state of the here and now.

I have practiced meditation before, and experienced vivid out-of-body experiences. I felt like I knew how to achieve a meditative state. But in that moment, meditation was not achieved, it was unveiled.

In traditional meditation, one often follows specific techniques and practices to enter a meditative state. These methods may involve focusing on the breath, focusing on sound, repeating mantras, or visualizing certain images. The goal is to quiet the mind, achieve inner stillness, and reach an altered state of consciousness.

However, in the presence of the fire and its ambiance, I found myself in a profound meditation that transcended my prior experiences.

It was the very essence of meditation that has revealed itself to me from within and not achieved from the outside. At that moment I realized that meditation needs no technique and no practice, as it is not a method that can lead somewhere. Meditation is the most basic state of our being when we just pause, take a break from the play of thought and perception.

The practice of meditation, mostly in Western cultures, is in a way a trick to get you out of meditation, because it is like trying to obtain something you already inherently have. It is like trying to find yourself, it can't be done, wherever you go —you are always there, so how can you find yourself? Every step you take towards yourself, you will find yourself there again. So in the same way, meditation is inherent, it is not a state achieved but rather unveiled.

That being said, I certainly think that this kind of understanding can be attained through practicing different methods of meditation. Despite its simplicity, this realization can come across as more advanced in its nature. This is why training oneself to look for the state of meditation is important, because it can eventually lead to the understanding that it is not a state one can find, but rather a default state that has always been there.

This is very similar to Zen and Buddhist teachers that send their students to go and look for themselves, mainly to get them to understand that it can't be done, and when they are so desperate and tired of looking for themselves, they finally get it.

CHAPTER 7:

THE VOICE

Let me clarify by saying that the inner voice I experienced was not akin to an external voice one might typically imagine. Instead, it manifested as a sensation that emerged from within my very being. Just as hunger doesn't necessitate verbal confirmation like: "Am I hungry?" it becomes an intrinsic knowledge. Similarly, feelings of pain, love, and other intense states are felt in every fiber of one's being, requiring no explicit articulation.

And so the voice inside me said,

"In your imaginary concept of yourself in this life, you are under an illusion. It is a dream of separation between you and others, the "play" of the many inside the dream of the one. The separation is by yourself so you can look at yourself from a distance.

For this separation to fulfill and sustain, you are absorbed in dissociation from "the other." The separation is conditioned by your body-mind that creates an illusory image of the world, based on the senses of the body-mind.

"Why do we suffer?" I asked.

The voice inside me replied,

"Heaven and Hell are mental states. They are inherent to the nature of the mind, intrinsic attributes of the mind, and the framework and the context of the mind. Your authentic essence is neither Heaven nor Hell; suffering is alien to you, only the illusory you endures it. You lack nothing in any form or concept, and you are boundless; you have never been born, and you will never perish. Thus, you exist within the entirety of life, within all beings. And in all beings, you are the same singular entity. Pain or pleasure are mere interpretations of the mind; they are unrelated to reality.

The nature of your thoughts is driven by the force that preserves the illusion of separation between you and the world that appears outside of you. Fear creates the notion of lack, void or no fulfillment.

A meaning to life, is a concept that the mind creates, looking to fill the void. But there is no void; it is the nature of illusion to create such a void. The human experience is like a dream, the void that you are trying to fill is already full: it is you.

Fear is an illusion, a perception that keeps you away from yourself and from your individual potential as the human being you happen to be right now. You are always in the center of your life experience, watching the tides of thought going up and down, up and down. Observe how they come and go and leave no trace behind. There is nowhere to follow or seek them out. In their origins, they are made of illusion, made of mind.

Understand that thoughts are illusory, and as such, they are self-righteous in design and can imitate your own self, making them difficult to identify. Don't try to argue with thoughts, as this will only give them more power over you. It's the nature of illusions. The inner conflict in your mind is the power of thought taking over. To stop the conflict—disengage, even if you think you can resolve it completely. Simply acknowledge any thought and let it pass."

"What should one do to serve the experience of individuality as a human being?" I asked.

"No sacrifice should be made besides self-love, self-devotion, and admiration for the gift of life.

It is merely a play, a dream, and there is no one around to congratulate you or punish you.

The true nature of creation is spontaneity, and the everflow of pure awareness. Don't waste your time on fears; be a complete and realized human by following your individual true nature - it is the same nature of your heart."

I would ask questions, and sometimes an answer would come forth. Sometimes there was silence, and gradually the voice went back to where it came from and took its rest inside my heart-mind.

The Magic Truck experience turned all my intellectual understanding into a vivid reality, a self-evident presence of truth. I was a child again, I understood with intuition once more.

Many great thinkers, philosophers, spiritual teachers, and scientists that are concerned with explaining the nature of reality, awareness, or consciousness, have explained this in many ways. It was always close, but still just beyond the grasp of my understanding as a self evident experience.

Before this experience, my search for answers to the most important question: "Who am I?" was partly answered by these great men and women, but only intellectually and not experimentally or self-evidently.

And this is not, in any way, disrespect for them and their notions. In fact, if it wasn't for them, I would not have made the journey towards self-inquiry and would not possess sufficient tools to unpack the mystery of my experience.

CHAPTER 8:

MASKS

Everything that I have gained in search of meaning in life, I will share with you in a rather simple way. As I stated at the beginning of this book, I am just an ordinary guy; I have no scientific background nor am I a religious preacher or a mystic. I encourage you not to take my words as truth because they will lead you away from your own true self. One cannot find oneself outside of self. You are it, you are already whole, a complete and realized being, but you just fail to realize it behind the mask of who you think you are - the not realized human being. It is not to be grasped by the mind alone, sometimes, when something is so close to you, it can go undetected, unacknowledged. And thus, I offer my knowledge to you through the art of storytelling, employing metaphors and presenting paradoxes. I'm using the power of words to transcend mere words, and that's the essential insight you should take away while reading this book, or any book for that matter. As I mentioned earlier, words are not reality, they merely point to reality. Our conditioning to describe reality through words has led us to overlook the fact that reality isn't composed of words.

To find your true nature, think through the complicated, unanswered questions that most of society left behind and experiment with what you find until it's self evident. Don't be satisfied with blind belief alone, because the other side of blind belief is doubt, and you will never feel complete or whole as long as you have doubt.

Be concerned with it. Be thirsty and the water of knowledge will pour down on you. But remember that, although it may involve techniques and intellectual discourses, methods, and practices, the actual experience of realization will eventually have nothing to do with any of that. So, by all means, do not take the technique or discourse so seriously, solely view them as practical advice, or a useful map.

Self-inquiry is totally individual and may be understood in three minutes or thirty years. It depends mostly on the distrust of your current point of view and your current knowledge of the reality you are aware of right now.

Trust the universe, although it has become popular these days to make fun of such a statement. I would argue to the contrary.

Trusting the universe would be the smartest option one can bet on. Just look around you: the sun rises every morning by itself, Spring arrives, flowers bloom, water flows, and wind blows, all on their own, all for billions of years.Humanity, and that includes you, came out of this universe and all living beings— they are the result of the works of the universe.

I would argue that if there was something trustworthy in life, it would be the universe. The only real thing we know is the experience that we are who we are, and this is a direct act of the universe.

Our awareness of that is the medium through which we experience everything, and in the same way of duality - the experience and the experiencer are one. There is no difference between you and your experience, and once you have understood this, you have understood it all.

For the sake of the self-inquiry experiment, engage in it. Consistently question your viewpoints on reality and examine it from a fresh perspective—the evidence of your experiences.

Don't worry, if you don't like it, you can go back to your own reality anytime. It's waiting for you with arms wide open.

There are not many facts that we truly know about ourselves, although some we might know on the intellectual level or on the level of blind belief. What we can know for sure is only what is self-evident to us, the simplest thing we know: we are aware, alive, here, now. Or in other words, we know that we know.

So, who are you then?

You might say "John Smith," but "John Smith" is a name that was given to you. Although it is your name, it is merely a name like any other. You can even change it if you like.

You might say a human being, but a human being is just a race, a life form like any other life forms you find on this planet. This is not you; it is only a description of your appearance and life pattern.

You might say a person, but a person is a social concept. In fact, the origin of the word "person" is from the Greco-Roman "persona," meaning that from which the sound (sona) comes. The word persona was used to name the masks in plays in a drama. So, when you are referring to yourself by the word "person", you are actually calling yourself a mask or an actor. Isn't that a curious thing?

You might say, "Me, I'm me," but who is that me? What is the experience of "me" or "I"? Do you know it? If so, in what sense? Can you locate it somewhere?

When you attempt to describe the experience of "I," you will quickly realize that all you are doing is attaching qualities that people have proposed to you over the years or that have been described by your five senses. These are all ideas of yourself. But all of them have concepts and forms, and they are not really you, because one can see that these qualities come and go, ever-changing. Someone who was once young and beautiful eventually becomes old and deformed. Someone who was once powerful eventually becomes powerless and needs the help of others to survive.

Everything you can describe is coming and going all the time. Thus, it limits the concept of what you would call "I" because if you attribute concepts of any kind, you are putting boundaries of physical and metaphysical concepts on yourself. But think it through and examine it. Can you describe a limit to your awareness or experience of yourself or even locate it? Where are you right now anyway? A black hole inside your invisible head? Or are you formless, borderless?

It is like saying, "I'm just an ordinary person." But if you want to insult someone, just tell them, "You are ordinary," and see how they respond.

It is true that I did present myself as an ordinary guy in this book, but it's just a manner of speaking, a way of language. Me and you, are not ordinary in any way.

Inside ourselves, we feel extraordinary, the center of the universe. And in fact, this is absolutely true. Every one of us is now located in the center of the universe, the center of the human experience.

Some would say, "Well, it's a phenomenon of nature—a scientific method of evolution—and a part of the body or the mind, a thing called matter, things or stardust..."

As part of natural human progress, profound ideas emerge from the fields of neuroscience, physics, psychology and philosophy. These ideas present arguments that challenge our conventional perception of reality. According to these notions, consciousness is not a mere byproduct of the brain or any material entity. Instead, matter is perceived as a projection of consciousness from the mind's perspective.

The activity of consciousness is represented to us as matter through our five senses and perception. The world we experience as the outside world, is the interpretation of our body-mind, of the vast activity of consciousness that doesn't exist as such in reality, and only perceived as such from our body-mind disassociated point of view. Meaning, that what you perceive as things, or matter are mental, not physical activities, just like in dreams.

Imagine that you, as an individual, are akin to a separated self: an imaginary construct created by your mind. In this view, matter appears as the outer manifestation of consciousness, creating the illusion that matter is outside of the reality you call yourself, outside of your skin or what you assume yourself to be.

One might contemplate the cascading layers of existence: Is it possible that you, the conscious being capable of feeling; loving; touching; seeing; and creating, could emerge as a byproduct of the brain? The brain, in turn, is considered the product of the body, and the body, in its intricate complexity, is said to originate from the arrangement of elements known as matter.

But here lies the intriguing question: Are you truly a byproduct of rock, water, and fire—mere elements of the physical world? This idea proposes that the underlying intelligence resides within every rock, piece of wood, drop of water, and speck of matter, capable of engendering the miraculous phenomena we call consciousness and awareness. And of course, no one has ever found consciousness in matter and pointed it out as a location.

The absence of empirical evidence to substantiate this claim of the material world model, as scientific exploration has never revealed matter as the creator of consciousness, nor does it appear likely to do so in the future as it has no grounds for this theory. It seems paradoxical for something that lacks awareness itself to be the predecessor of consciousness.

Despite the lack of scientific validation, this idea of the physical/material world finds its place in the hearts of most people today as they seem to trust the superficial knowledge they are fed with. The other point of view of reality resonates with those who perceive consciousness as the foundation of reality, shaping the fabric of matter into existence by our sensory organs.

Dreams offer a glimpse into the power of consciousness, as it crafts landscapes without any material input, thus, creating a physical appearance that can objectively be understood as a mental activity. No one is surprised by that fact every morning when waking up from a dream, we just go about our day.

So, one might question the notion of being a byproduct of matter when the experiences within dreams suggest an alternative perspective where consciousness, the ultimate architect, manifests the material realm.

In your dreams, your brain activity could manifest as people, streets, buildings, cars, flowers, and everything else you encounter in dreams. Have you ever witnessed the opposite? Has matter ever transformed into the mental realm? Have you ever observed a rock evolving into a thought? In dreams, you may have seen rocks, but they were comprised of mental activity rather than physical substance. Hence, constructing an argument around a material world is challenging, while creating a concept of a mental world that better elucidates the field of science is considerably more straightforward.

In your dreams, are there no "real things"? Can you open a door? Can you walk on solid ground? Feel cold or warm? Can you see landscapes? Is it believable enough when you are dreaming? Sure, it is.

The dream compels most of us to believe it to be real. From our dreamed character's point of view, reality as we know it is nothing but a dream and vice versa. In other words, what is real?

So ask yourself, what is this stuff in your dreams made of? It looks and feels like everyday matter or things. So is it? Obviously not, it is made of mental activity that is interpreted by the mind as physical activity.

The model of a material world often leads to a common misconception: that matter's measurability makes it inherently real. However, this perspective is limited and fails to consider an alternative explanation.

Let's imagine measuring the length of a shadow cast by an object. By using scientific tools, we can precisely determine the dimensions of the shadow, providing us with valuable information about the object that casts it. Yet, it's essential to recognize that the shadow itself is merely a representation of the object's activity; it is not the actual object. In fact, what you are seeing is the absence of light in a certain spot. As such, validating the shadow's properties does not confer any true reality upon it. While we can draw conclusions based on the shadow's quantities, we cannot extract the shadow and tuck it into our pockets. It remains a mere reflection of the object's presence.

In this analogy, physical matter functions similarly to the shadow. While we can measure and analyze material entities, they serve as representations of the activity of the mind. From the point of view of the mind, matter is a way to convey a perception, similarly to the activity of dreams. Just as the shadow reveals insights into the object that casts it, matter provides information about the workings of the mind.

Like the shadow, matter lacks an inherent reality of its own. It is a projection, a manifestation of the mind from a certain point of view.

The essence of this perspective lies in recognizing that the true nature of reality is consciousness itself as the real medium through which all of the manifested world exists, including yourself as a conscious being.

Matter, in all its measurable forms, is but a reflection of the vastness and intricacy of consciousness. While we can perceive matter, anticipate events based on its properties, and draw conclusions from its behavior, it remains secondary to the underlying consciousness that gives rise to it.

If you go back to your dreams, the time and space in which the dream character exists are not real time and space. They are made of the illusion of the dream. For example, you can spend a whole day in a dream while being asleep for a few minutes. The time and space of your dreamed character were not real, the only true underlying reality of the dream was the dreamer—who was you. There was no matter, no time, and no space. Just you.

The biggest clue we get from dreams is the ability of the mind to disassociate the character from the rest of the dream. That is to say, when you dream, the mind disassociates your metaphysical presence in the dream as "you" from the rest of the dream while the "other things" in your dream are as much "you" as the dreamed character. This disassociation is the key understanding of self-inquiry and the power of the illusion that the mind creates.

Assume that it's exactly what is happening right now, that you are in a dream

Why? Because it is self-evident to be a quality of the mind to disassociate "you and other", and appear equally real between the waking state we call reality and the dream state.

When asleep, you think it to be real, and when not asleep, you think it to be real. So what is real?

We live in a mental world, this is why sugar pills can cure medical conditions, placebo surgeries can heal knee pain and hypnosis can treat physical illnesses. Any of this should not occur in a physical world, but it does, in abundance.

A more valid approach to reality should be based on the actual experience of existence rather than on a theory of existence. In such a point of view, we could all say that no one has ever found matter or "things" that were outside of consciousness.

The only reason that experience ever happens for us is the mind, and we are all aware that we are aware. This is the most basic fact we know.

Most people look at the big questions of life superficially, but I encourage you to take another look at it. The people in your dreams, who are they if not you? The "things" in your dreams, what are they if not you?

So, who are you then?

CHAPTER 9:

TAT TVAM ASI

To grasp the complete idea of unity, or the hidden connection between everything, you should revisit the separation we explored earlier: black and white, young and old, light and darkness. They all imply each other, serving as references to one another, and they cannot exist without their counterparts—their duality.

A white dot on a 2D white background doesn't truly remain distinct, as it cannot be differentiated; for the dot or the background to create each other as distinct elements, they must possess different qualities of color. Otherwise, they become indistinguishable. If the only reality of the dot is the white background, it loses its significance as it lacks a reference point, and the background loses its quality as a background as well, because there is nothing else but white, so there is no background. As the dot emerges with varying colors from the background, the two come into existence. Look for yourself and explore whether these things are genuinely separate or if they are merely plotting to appear separated. Though they may seem distinct, they are, in fact, the same because they can't exist otherwise.

Could it be that your belief of separation between "you and other" is just a perception that has been mistaken for reality? Conduct an experiment; hold a stick and say, "This is one end, and this is the other end." You can even give each end a name, a quality, a quantity, or even a royal title to each end of the stick if you really wish. But isn't that still a whole stick you are holding?

Can it be that the game of division and separation made you forget about the whole stick?

Your imaginary division of one end of the stick and the other end created the illusion of two ends of the same stick, thus you have created a difference, a separation. Can you see that in other aspects of life?

Is the division of the day into separate events a true reality? Or is it a collective agreement we use in language? If you believe time is constructed of events, then how would you explain the sequence and timing of these events? Did the occurrence of wind bring about the event we call "wave"? Or did the ocean bring forth the initial "water" event? Or did the earth pave the way for this to occur? Alternatively, going deeper, could it all be traced back to the big bang. If that's the case, each event could conceivably be logically traced back to the moment of the big bang, and thus the entirety of all events could be attributed to it. But surely we don't think about it this way. Hence, we often overlook the fact that time isn't composed of separate events; instead, it flows like water, constituting a singular occurrence—the continuous event of "now."

In the same way, feeling good is just a reference to feeling bad. How would you know the difference between good and bad without experiencing one of them? To know one thing, you must know the other, to know the one, you must know the many.

Observe it in your own experience. Look for the separation and the hidden connection everywhere. When you find that all in creation is dual and depends on each other you will then raise far more profound questions: What is dual to me? What is dual to God? What is dual to the ultimate reality? That is to say, if it had a dual quality to it, it wouldn't be ultimate, it would have a border or a limit.

So if God is dual, there must be another aspect or reference to God. And that makes God… not very Godly, less than God.

For the problem of duality, the Eastern traditions presented the understanding of non-duality. Meaning not this and not that, Neti Neti (Sanskrit : नेति नेति), the thing that cannot relate to anything and can just be regarded as "not this, not that." It needs no reference and thus cannot be described. It has no form thus it is formless; it has no quantities thus it can't be measured.

In this they mean God, in this they mean you—the real you, the atman, or the soul. You, God, The Universe, or whatever you would like to call it, is not measurable, can't be referenced, and can't be described by language.

The sole means to perceive God is to be God, because neither you or God could be an object to your own knowledge. By this, I don't imply that you alone are the sole deity capable of performing miracles, commanding admiration, and demanding obedience.

In this context, you're equally a manifestation of the divine, just as anyone else is.

If you were to become another being and step into its consciousness, you would still be you, all beings are you, but you can experience them one at a time, and this is the big blessing of this creation—the one that plays the many and experiences itself as an individual. Remember your dreams and you will see that this is the same experience—you can be someone that is not the physical you and still feel as yourself, the only self there is.

The real borderless and shapeless God that is each and every one of us has no lack and no need for anything, it is already everything. There is no purpose that needs to be fulfilled as it will contradict the very essence of a God.

So why did we conceive the idea of a grandfather type, bearded, serious God figure? Why did we construct our cultures around this concept?

We derive the idea of this "Human God" and the world as an object created by God from the ancient Hebrews. In the bible, God created the universe just like an engineer or a mechanic that built a machine and gave it life, and that makes God a cosmic mechanic. This kind of world that was suggested by the ancient Hebrews, is fully controlled by God like the Big Brother in George Orwell's book *1984*, a totalitarian regime, a monarchy, where the poor disciples live under surveillance 24/7 all the time.

But it's not just that. According to this belief, everything you do or even think in secret is registered somewhere, and when you die, you will face your sins or reap your rewards. If you have been a good boy or girl, you will get rewarded and forever rejoice while other sinners burn in hell for eternity—spooky indeed.

Well, if that were the case, life would become an incredibly terrifying experience. Just think about living in a state where you're always being judged, assessed, and living under the constant shadow of threats. It's hard to even imagine how nightmarish such a situation could be.

Set aside the obvious reasoning that we don't have any evidence for this whatsoever besides some old books from the times when people lived by standards and ideas that would seem absurd today.

What's even worse is that it doesn't make sense from a true divine point of view. The model of God as a great human, a king and a judge is not a real God whatsoever.

The logic behind this perspective seems to serve the purpose of enabling a specific group of individuals to gain control over others, using the threat of Hell as a means of obedience. This framework of belief reduces God to little more than a potent human figure—someone who is wrathful, envious, and possessive, yet also capable of exhibiting a nurturing, paternal demeanor. Does this description truly resemble a divine being? Or does it perhaps resemble more closely a human who conceived the concept of God? Contemporary psychology would categorize such a personality as a classic example of an abuser.

In these traditions, God is often referred to as the "King of kings" or "The one true lord," among other titles. These titles serve as symbolic representations of the paradigm that humanity embraced thousands of years ago. It's challenging to imagine God as resembling a king or a lord, given that these designations are inherently transient and limited—qualities that do not align with the nature of God as the ultimate reality, which is surely boundless.

The notion of God as a lord or king resonated with the ethos of those eras. Nonetheless, it's evident that this construct is a human creation—an embodiment of authority and control over others. Being identified as the representative of the "King of Kings" grants one with immense importance, and this is why people that dress holy are treated as holy, it's just a social game we play and pretend that it is a serious business.

But isn't it plausible that the ultimate God possesses a sense of humor? After all, why would humor even exist if not for that purpose? As a result, the sensitivity of religious topics to humor and the subsequent reactions appear rather ironic when considering the broader perspective.

The alternative worldview is rooted in science. This approach presents an entirely mechanistic model of the world, akin to an engineering blueprint. This model emerged as a reaction from those who grew tired of God as the "Big Brother".

In this model, there is no God. That is, there is no boss, and everything that exists is nothing but a mere chance: a big cosmic mess that somehow created all of this magic we perceive, including our consciousness.

The mechanical point of view dismisses God but keeps the rest without much change.

There is still the cosmic law that is referred to as "matter" or the natural law of the universe, but there is no lawmaker anymore, no boss.

Ask yourself, if everything is mere coincidence, a one-in-a-trillion chance that you and everything else here will fade away with time, what is the point of going about your life? Isn't that a drag as well? What can you possibly achieve in this model of the universe? After all, you will die, so will everyone else you know and love, and all your belongings and achievements will vanish.

So why bother? Who will remember you in a thousand years? A million years? No one.

If this is a model you are following, you are positioning yourself as a machine, including the part that thinks about it. Does that not strike you as bizarre and counterintuitive to your experience of the world which is rich and meaningful? Does this feel like a mechanical world to you? Do you actually feel like a machine?

So in this model, people are unknowingly practicing the same absurdity while thinking that they are more sophisticated than the people that obey the big boss.

Well, for this model we don't have any evidence whatsoever, and like the belief in God as a mechanic, the belief in the world as a machine is simply a belief as well.

Why not attempt to perceive the world from the only viewpoint we can truly understand and validate? Why not observe the world through the lens of personal experience?

Why not look at nature and see that we are not a puppet in the hands of a great human God, nor are we a machine that exists because of a cosmic mistake, but rather, we are it: the universe itself, an extension, an expression, a point of view of the vast, borderless universe.

For that model, we can find evidence in our own experience without anyone pointing it out to us. Just look at yourself. Are you not one with everything else? How could you possibly know something without other things to refer to? How could you be you without others? As others need you, you need others; you need things and things need you. Thus, you are one with them, an organism that is one with the environment. And that is to say, you are the original one, looking at yourself from a limited point of view, playing the human game.

"Tat tvam asi," means in Sanskrit, "You are it!"

If you push aside your ideas from the models I have described and think about a metaphor of a tree, you will get it.

Take a look at the fruit of a tree. It is special, colorful, beautiful, full of taste and purpose. But isn't it the original tree you are looking at? Isn't the fruit an extension, an expression of the tree? It's not in any way separated from the tree: it is the tree. Although from the fruit's perspective, the tree might appear dull, not very intelligent, and sometimes even hostile. Does this ring a bell? It is just as we see the world outside ourselves as humans.

For us, the border of "I" is our skin, and everything outside of our skin is therefore related as "other". But aren't we the fruit of the universe? Can't we see that although we look different we are still the continuous process of the source? The fingers look different from our ears, the liver looks different from the nose, but it is all one body. Thus, the appearances of differences are merely perceptions of separation and in fact, they are one.

If you embark on the journey of looking for yourself, you will eventually realize that your own presence becomes elusive, nowhere to be found.

It's almost as if you were in such proximity, yet too near to perceive. You can sense it, and yet, your essence remains intangible. How can one locate oneself? After all, if you were to achieve such a task, wouldn't that result in the existence of two distinct manifestations of yourself?

If you were indeed to discover your true self, wouldn't that imply the existence of two distinct versions of you? How could such a scenario even be feasible? The only way this would make sense is that you would find out that who you thought you were, was not real.

As you deepen into the quest of self-inquiry, more layers of reality will peel away and you will begin to see what you were always looking for was never there in the first place. You have always been looking from the point of view of the illusory self, and this is why there was nothing to be found.

How can one be so sure about the "self" being eternal? Or the self as God?

Well, think about the questions that arose in this chapter. Are you a form or formless in essence? And when you see that you are formless, can formlessness arrive from somewhere? Can it be created?

A formlessness cannot be limited by any form or concept, otherwise it wouldn't be formless. This is a simple way of understanding who you really are. And if that is the case, you were always here, not created by a boss or by cosmic chance.

You can always describe the formless once it is manifested as a form. But when the form is gone, all description is lost.

It is like the difference in the appearance of the form of a living human being, and the body they will leave behind when they die.

That body has the same form, but you know it's not the same man or woman anymore. So how would you describe them now? They still have the body form, yes, but the "thing" that gave life to the body form, gave qualities such as laughter, drama, and love was always formless, and when it went away, it left behind a form, but not itself, thus, it was never created, and it was always and for eternity free of limitation. This is your true nature, whoever you might be, or think you are: you are it—"Tat tvam asi."

Give space to your own intuition, your heart-mind, to investigate the most unsolved mystery of the universe, of yourself.

Be open to the idea that you are, by definition, safe. If you accept that no harm can come to the real you, and that you are limitless, borderless, formless, and shapeless; then you will experience it.

In one way or another, your true nature will dance and express itself, like electricity through its temporary host.

Be willing to look at the universe from a new point of view, free from previous misconceptions, for the sake of the experiment and the discovery of the self.

I recall a childhood joke that summarizes this idea, and it goes like this:

John walks down the street and sees Andy looking for something under a streetlight. "What are you doing?" asks John. "I'm looking for my car keys," Andy replies.

"Where did you lose them?" inquires John.

"About two blocks from here," Andy states.

"So why are you looking for the keys here?" John asks. Surprised, Andy answers, "Well, it's dark over there, and here I can see thanks to the streetlight."

So even if you think that you found light elsewhere, outside of yourself, you will still not find the key to your truth, as it cannot be found in a different place from where you are standing right now. In other words, you are already yourself, just hiding behind your persona. So simply shine a light back on yourself, focus your attention to the source of your experience and you will see this as self-evident.

CHAPTER 10:

THE BOOKKEEPER

One night, I found myself standing on the balcony when a sudden insight struck me. I fixed my gaze upon a specific spot on the street below, and a thought occurred to me: how can I ensure that I remember this particular spot? Naturally, the answer seemed to be that if I continued to stare for a prolonged period, meticulously absorbing every detail from side to side, including the surrounding noises, scents, and patterns of light, eventually it would be imprinted in my memory. Yet, then a new question arose: where exactly do I store this memory? Where does this repository, which I frequently rely upon, reside? What precisely constitutes the process of memory, and how can I retrieve it when needed? These thoughts inspired me to develop an unusual theory concerning the genuine essence of our identity.

Let's assume that the core of our existence is pure subjectivity, that is to say - we know only ourselves. As we come into this human existence, we lack awareness of anything beyond our individual subjective experience, this is why babies don't care about your feelings, they do what they do, they are—pure subjectivity. The body-mind, which in essence is a complex dance of vibrations, attempts to comprehend our subjective encounters with the world and translating them into the concept of time, space and meaning. Wait, what?

I understand that this might sound a bit unconventional, but allow me to delve deeper into the concept. Take a moment to contemplate the following notion: If your memory were entirely erased, resulting in a loss of your identity, what would remain? It would be nothing but pure subjectivity—the experience of your own self. There would be no words, thoughts, or interpretations. This phenomenon also occasionally occurs in dreams, where the dream's setting consists of nothing but pure subjectivity, even without any prior recollections of the dream's preceding events, your existence persists without issue.

If so, this is the exact mechanism of the illusory self. Let me explain it in terms of what I call - "The bridge" concept.

Think of your breathing right now, just do it— stop for a moment and breathe in, hold, and breathe out. You did it ? great! Now stop breathing, can you do that?

You will find out that this is impossible to do, but why? It seems that when we don't think about it, breathing just happens by itself without any active effort from your side, but when you do think about it - it acts as if breathing needs your attention, otherwise you will die.

Notice, that after some time of intentional breathing, the breathing will continue without you, but it will only happen unnoticeably, that is to say - when you are not paying any attention to it. And after a while you suddenly recognize that the breathing did its own thing without you. So how is that possible? This is "The bridge".

"The bridge" is the metaphorical point where you, and the illusory you meet. It is not only the breath - but far beyond that. "The bridge" is a secret doorway to your subconscious mind that is the gatekeeper of the illusion you call "I".

When these bridges become apparent, you can see that your body-mind is actively trying to convince you that you are it. To feel any of its pain or to participate in any of its thoughts. This is not because the body-mind is some evil entity, not at all. This is the mechanism of the game, the illusion. The body mind is the ultimate servant, you can do just about whatever you want with it on a physical level, like many athletes do and on the mental level, like many great artists, scientists, entrepreneurs and great teachers do.

When we are born, our body-mind is on a mission to communicate with us, to be us and mimic us. In fact, it does it so well that with time, we are totally mixed up and hooked on the idea that this is actually who we really are. But if you try to stop breathing or stick your hand into fire, you will find out that the body-mind has self survival instincts that have nothing to do with you, it has its own desires. If you examine this theory in your life, you will see that the desires of the body-mind are not your desires, at least most of the time. You want to eat, you want to rest, you want to breathe, you want to sleep, you want this and that—but do you really?

And so, one could ask, am I a puppet of the body-mind? Or is the body-mind a puppet of mine?

Let me suggest that it's neither, it's rather a musical instrument, a play, and like any play or musical instrument - you need the skills to play it, otherwise it will be awful.

In this regard, the subconscious mind is basically blind and naive. Why? Look at your own life and see that the ideas you have about yourself are emotions that your body-mind picked up when you were just a child. Your fears and dramas are based on the registered events that your subconscious mind has kept in its books.

Why is that? Because the medium through which the subconscious mind is processing the input of your pure subjectivity is mainly the medium of emotions. The greater the emotion, the more bookkeeping is done.

As previously discussed, in a state of pure subjectivity, you lack pre-existing knowledge or understanding of anything, yet it is through this very state that you come to comprehend everything. Reality is not made of words, it is made of reality, and so your input to the subconscious mind is not verbal, it is emotional.

The verbal art, or words - are nothing but symbols of reality, they are not in any way the actual real thing. If you really explore this idea, you will see that words are a complexity of the basic word "that". All we do with words is point out a reality that is beyond the word itself, it is the basic sound that babies make when they point to something and say "tha." They are saying "that", and so do we, but in a multiplicity of patterns. You can point to anything and use the word "that", and it will be equally correct as any other word. The word water is the same as pointing at water and saying: "that." and in this way, we are just complicating reality with symbols of reality, as the word water, as discussed earlier in the book, would not make your thirst go away.

Think of the subconscious mind as a blind bookkeeper, a registrar that keeps any records of your experiences of here and now, processes them and fires them back at you. When this happens, the illusion of time and space is created, as if it happened somewhere in the past as separate events, but in fact, everything happens here and now, there is no past whatsoever. The illusion of the past, and as a byproduct - the concept of the future are the works of the subconscious mind, the great bookkeeper, and as long as you subscribe to this, you're hooked.

So what then? It's not as though anyone has direct access to this subconscious mind, right? Well, we actually do. It might not be straightforward and easy at first, but nonetheless, let me introduce the concept I call "The Garden".

CHAPTER 11:

THE GARDEN

Imagine yourself as a gardener, your experience of life is the labor of gardening, and your subconscious mind is the garden. From a very young age, without knowing, you were gardening.

Seeds of happiness, joy, love, fear, and trauma were planted and began to grow. As they matured, these seeds transformed and manifested into the reality you are experiencing now, a reality that bears little resemblance to the original seeds. In other words, a seed of fear that you planted due to that scary dog trying to bite you when you were seven years old could easily manifest as a fear of meeting new people.. Why? It's complicated to say, but in essence, the seeds you plant grow in an environment with others seeds and they have influence over each other, so when they grow, they change.

The tricky part is that the garden of your mind isn't accessible to you in the same way as the garden at your home.. It is a subtle garden, a magical garden. There is only one door in, and no visible door out. The input you send to your mental garden can only return as the output of your mind, in the form of thoughts or emotions. This means that you can't simply reach back and extract what is unnecessary to you.

To understand the garden is to delve deep into your experiences and identify the seeds you once unknowingly planted—much like my LSD cat experience.

Once the connection was established between the pain I felt as a child from losing my cat and the cat allergy I had developed, the pain magically disappeared. This occurred because I had identified the seed and recognized its nature, understanding that the cat allergy was merely a seed of pain and suffering that manifested as a physical condition.

Similarly, numerous expressions of your mind today—reflected in your thought patterns and your system of judgment regarding good and bad, beauty and ugliness, right and wrong, and all the other elements of what you term "Taste"—constitute the original seeds that have blossomed into mature trees within your enchanting garden.

It is a good practice to search for those seeds, understand their origins and accept them, love them, and forgive them. This way, they are just seeds of illusion, a part of the game, and not the core of your personality, which, whatever it may be right now, can change.

To become a genuine gardener, master the art of self-talk, sow new seeds, and craft your fresh garden. Yet, exercise caution. Just as a real garden can't handle too many changes at once without disturbing the soil, practice patience and make gradual adjustments.

Don't force planting seeds that are not in harmony with the rest of the garden yet. It is the art of creating a harmonious garden, not the art of forcing. If you have no money at all, don't tell yourself that you will become a billionaire tomorrow. This seed will not see life in your garden, no matter how hard you try to plant it.

Compel your garden step by step as a practice, as an art. Plant seeds that can be accepted in the magical soil, step by step in accordance with the garden you have right now.

This is the essence of manifestation. It is like a gym in which you build the perfect body—you don't show up one day and push beyond your limits, you will get burned out and injured, and that will probably be the end of it, and thus you might think that the gym is merely a fanciful wishful thinking exercise.

In the case of the garden, it is a mental gym, but it works according to the exact same principle: the principle of building from the ground up, learning, and making a routine out of it, a mastery, a ritual. If your garden is totally messed up, start by nurturing it with love, forgiveness, acceptance—and build from there.

One could wonder, how exactly do we plant these seeds? Well, from my perspective, our intelligence suggests that understanding how things function can often be achieved through reverse engineering. Similarly, if we consider the garden as a representation of our interpreted emotions, it follows that the most potent method to plant seeds involves infusing them with emotion, engaging in self-affirming thoughts, and having unwavering self-belief. Use a short daily ritual that will keep you mindful throughout the day, that will help you stay in a good mental shape.

Find what drives your positive emotions and use them to plant seeds. Feeling love? Take a moment and say to yourself - I love myself. Feel lucky and happy? Say to yourself - I am lucky, and more luck is coming my way, and in this moment - you have planted a seed.

But as discussed, planting seeds, like planting real-life seeds, is not enough. Seeds need nurturing, care and love. And so, in the same manner, do the same thing to your seeds, to your garden. Make time to take care of it every day, at least a decent amount of time that you feel ok with. If you leave it to grow without nurturing, it will die, and only the strongest seeds will prevail. What are the strongest seeds? You already know the answer to that as your life experience has shown you time and again.

Fear and negative emotions are the most potent, fast growing seeds in your garden, and to make a case for it - let me share a simple example.

You walk down the street when suddenly a stranger stops you and says: "Hi, you look beautiful today, I love you." How would you feel about it?

Mostly you will be uncomfortable and surely you will not jump and hug this stranger.

But if a different stranger would stop you from walking and say: "You are one ugly looking human", how would you react? Rage, violence, sadness?

So you see that seeds of negativity grow fast, but what if the loving stranger with the kind words would show up every day or so, and say more and more of these compliments? With time, you would learn to love this stranger, appreciate his words and even share some kind words back. So you see, positive seeds take longer to grow, but they grow if nurtured, and are sustained if you are mindful of them.

And so, this is the formula - plant seeds with positive emotions and nurture them until they have the natural power to grow and sustain. Seeds of fear, anger or any negative seeds - accept them, love them and forgive them. When you learn to do that, you will unlock the power of using bad energy for a good cause in the same way that one does in martial arts. In my own experience with martial arts, an important lesson I learned was to identify the mistakes my opponent made and convert them into opportunities for personal gain—this is the exact same technique.

CHAPTER 12:

KEYS

While I have clearly stated that the comprehension of one's true self cannot be solely captured by the intellect, it's crucial to acknowledge that the intellect is a magnificent and wondrous tool. "A great servant, but a lousy master," as it has been described by many throughout history.

So, in order to evoke the intellect and turn it into a brilliant servant, I will share my key understandings from my own experience that can help you navigate the high waters of life's ultimate quest.

I understand now more than ever the difficulty of realizing our true nature. Not because it is so hard, but because it is so simple. Simplicity is tricky due to our conditioning from birth, our learned concepts and truths about the reality we live in.

From the point of view of highly intellectual, material-minded individuals, it can be even more challenging because those types of minds conceptualize everything into unambiguous symbols that can be validated only by other symbols. They look for representations of reality instead of reality itself.

The conception of it all makes them believe less in intuition, and this is because their minds are heavily conditioned to believe and trust in a certain way.

In the same way, you trust your mobile phone to launch an app and believe the app to be real because it is working, it's alive. But the underlying reality of the app is a dance of binary digits on the screen, and so, the reality of the app is far more subtle than the appearance of the app on the phone's screen.

Although the app's interface corresponds with the phone's capabilities, it is certainly not the reality of your phone.

And so, the mobile phone is all there is to the app. The app is a temporary presence on the mobile phone's screen. The app corresponds with the qualities of the screen. But at all times, the underlying reality of the app is always the mobile phone's screen.

While you were interacting with your social app, you were looking at a black screen that had been temporarily populated with multiplicities of complicated variations, and you confused it with the phone's screen.

On the other hand, many spiritual people, from their point of view, can often get stuck in methods that have brought them to a certain point of profoundness, and they are afraid to break out of it or let it go.

One could argue that they are making the same mistake as their counterparts.

Individuals who engage in meditation to improve their circumstances often miss the essence of meditation, and similarly, those who pray can fall into the same misconception.

Nevertheless, immense beauty, elegance, and joy can be discovered in spiritual practices when they are pursued solely for the sake of joy. The self-improvement method of spirituality is a trap that almost never gets people out of the illusion cycle.

Don't get caught in the competition of "my method is better" or "my understanding is greater." There is no need for that.

Discover joy in practices, whether material or spiritual, and engage in them for the enjoyment they bring and the elegance they exhibit—similar to how you would approach any other game.

The realization of oneself, or the true nature of oneself, could be intellectually discussed in rational ways, but this is only an intellectual understanding and not the real deal.

Having said that, I truly think that intellectual thinking is a very powerful tool to create the right conditions for such an experience.

I would suggest the following: Don't look for the experience of your true nature, don't look for God. Try to understand the basics and let life flow. May it be a psychedelic trip, meditation, or a lovely Sunday morning stroll down the street, it can hit you anywhere. However, refrain from seeking it out obsessively.

The looking for, or investigation is that which creates the distance between "you and other" in the first place. It's like the inches that create the distance between the two imaginary ends of the same stick. As long as you try to use inches to describe or comprehend the stick, your quest will lead you astray.

It may sound counterintuitive to our goal-oriented minds - the minds that believe that everything can be obtained by force and willpower. However, it is completely the other way around. Nature is not forced, so why should you force it? Aren't you a manifestation of nature?

Close your eyes and take a stride inward, towards your very essence. Regardless of your efforts, you'll realize there's no separation between you and your own self. Similarly, seeking what you desire cannot be achieved through direct pursuit; however, it can be uncovered, for it already exists within you. It's an inherent aspect, obscured only by a veil that must be lifted in order for you to perceive it.

If I could offer you some advice, I would choose the method of storytelling and asking questions that will present a paradox or ignite the thirst for self-inquiry.

Turn your mind towards itself, the mind will take care of the rest.

To help get you started, I have prepared six keys. These keys are not the answer, they are only an invitation, a reminder, an instrument. Treat them as such.

**First key: Here is not a point in space,
now is not a point in time.**

It's a rather strange misconception that people
say, "Be here now," and refer to a point in space and
time, as if the meaning of it should refer to general
relaxation. The real point of "here and now" is to
break free from the limitations of time and space and
turn your attention to the limitless "here and now."

In order to understand "now," let's use a familiar
example. Take a look at any watch. The time on the
watch is represented by different hands. The hands
represent hours, minutes, and seconds. So, when you
are referring to the present moment, is it the thinner
hand that indicates it? Obviously not, otherwise, we
would live in a kind of world that turns the future
into the past every second, leaving you with no time
to be "now" because it's ever-changing.

How could one live in such a frantic "now" that
keeps changing every second? How can one grasp
the present moment if that moment ticks away all
of the time? Tick, tick, tick, tick....where are you in
reference to these ticks?

So, in other words, the "now" that is represented
on the watch is not at all the real "now." It's a classic

example of how we confuse language and symbols with reality.

Even when you have a memory of the past, and you say, "There is the past," where does the memory take place? Have you ever had a memory that did not arise in the "now"?

And so, the real "now" is not a point in time, it is a state of flow, the moment that is never bound by time, the eternal now.

In your experience, there is only "now." Yesterday was "now" and so will be tomorrow. As the saying goes, "Tomorrow never comes."

In order to understand "here," let's use our own experience. Have you ever experienced the sensation "there"? "There" is only an illusion that you perceive, or a symbol of reference in measuring distance. Once you are there, it becomes "here." In fact, you were never there at all, you were always "here." Wherever you go, you take yourself with you.

So, is "here" a point in space? No.

Refer to your own experience of "here and now" and take a fresh look at it. You will see that "now" is the interpretation of eternity from the point of view of the mind as time, and "here" is the interpretation

of infinity as space, the works of the great bookkeeper,
the subconscious mind.

Second key: The inner conflict

The most profound understanding I had during
my mushroom trip with the Tea of the Gods was that
thoughts and perceptions were coming and going, but
I was always present... watching them come and go.

And so, the question arises: How do thoughts
and perceptions affect us? Can we not resist or ignore
them?

Think of an illusion. What powers an illusion?
What defines the quality of an illusion?

The answer is that an illusion, on its own,
possesses no inherent power. An illusion lacks genuine
influence unless you grant it power. Our thoughts
and perceptions hold us hostage sometimes, giving
us anxiety, fear, stress, doubt, and other phenomena
that most of the time don't even occur in real life. So
how is that possible?

Well, the key lies in the fact that when a thought
or perception arises in consciousness, it is powerless
on its own; it's your attention that grants it power.
For instance, imagine walking down a dark street

alone. Suddenly, a thought emerges, "There might be someone behind me." In response, you either turn around to check or dismiss the notion. Yet, in that precise moment, you've granted power to the thought, allowing the sensation of "Someone is behind me" to persist.

Unfortunately, we cannot simply ignore these thoughts because "ignoring" is a different word for "recognizing." It's a duality. When you have recognized the thought, even for a fraction of a second, it's alive. Then, the mind will try to find a logical solution, a reason to ignore the thought on solid ground.

The thought might say, "There is no one behind me, no reason to get uptight." This is the essence of illusion, a trick.

The mind will try to analyze the situation that was triggered by thought. Or to put it in another way, you will try to convince yourself that you have made the right decision. A thought convincing a thought.

The trick of thought is that it's inherently self-righteous and will consider no argument as acceptable, even if the argument is verified and well-established.

The voices in your head will argue and argue, creating more noise and illusion. You might say that thought, in essence, works as the Devil's Advocate and is paid by the hour, so the more, the merrier.

If you understand the nature of your thoughts and perceptions, you can see that they are not you, they are only wonderful phenomena.

There are good and constructive thoughts that can drive you to create great things, and there are destructive thoughts that will bring you down or destroy you slowly until there is only fear and anxiety left.

Once you realize the nature of thought, you can choose which thoughts interest you and which thoughts are destructive. Don't ignore them, don't try to rationalize them with your mind. That, as I said before, creates the illusion.

So, remember, there is no method to convince the mind of anything. Not by logic and not by spiritual practice, only by the recognition of the game itself. Remember, thoughts are like birds: they just come and fly away.

If you are lured in, snap out of it upon recognition. Don't be hard on yourself because it's not you that is hard on yourself anyway, it's just another thought.

Third key: Love, forgive and let go

From my own experience, I have found that self-love is not at all a selfish thing. Well, at least not in a bad way as society propagates the idea of being selfish.

Let's have a look at the idea of self-love. What is it truly?

Well, everyone says that they love themselves, but do they really? I found out from my countless interactions with people that love is only granted to oneself under certain conditions. Meaning, that when people love themselves, they do that mostly when such a feeling is appropriate in their minds.

For example, if they did something right, or managed to accomplish a goal, they'll say, "I love myself today," or "I love this part of me," and so on. Is this real love? Or is it love under strict conditions?

True love for oneself can only be a state of total acceptance and forgiveness of all imperfections, past deeds, shame and guilt, like taking musical chances without the fear of failure. Love gives you the freedom to be yourself.

When you realize that these feelings and perceptions of yourself are just a functioning of your mind, only then can you truly love yourself without any logical reason.

Love yourself anyway, even if there are no "valid" reasons to do so. When I look at my children, I don't look for reasons to love them, I do it because it's fun. I like watching them do silly things, I like watching them live their lives, and I'm sure you can see that too in your own life, in your own examples of love.

I love my dog Teddy for no reason. In fact, if I looked for reasons, I would probably lose the idea of loving him because, essentially, there were no reasons in the first place. This perspective challenges societal norms, for we are conditioned from birth to associate love with specific conditions. This is rooted in our relationships with everyone. Do you love me? If so, I love you. If you don't do what I expect you to do, then I won't love you back – maybe I'll even hate you.

We often confuse love with its superficial understanding. True love has no reason, and this is the best part about it.

It is the same for forgiveness. Don't forgive just to feel better about yourself. Don't hide your agendas deep inside and act as if you truly forgive. This is just a manipulation of the mind, and you are only fooling yourself.

So why forgive?

You forgive because you deeply understand that all the anger or disappointment you might have inside you towards someone is, in fact, your own anger and disappointment, and it rarely has anything to do with the person you are attributing the anger or disappointment to.

What your mind interprets is only an expectation that things will work out under your terms, under total control. And when it doesn't, you feel angry or disappointed.

Control is not what you really want. Even the emperors and high kings of history recognized that control and power are more a curse than a blessing.

Many suffered and died when they achieved total control or the illusion of total control. What would you do if you were all power and mighty? Would you control everything for eternity? This is not the best idea as you will get bored soon enough.

Think it through. Is control a quality that could be attributed to the metaphor of God or the ultimate reality?

It is a quality of someone that is neither God nor the ultimate reality. God, or whatever name you want to call the higher power, already has it all. Control is not a quality that can exist in such a reality. It is just like saying that water needs to be wet as a quality or that light needs to shine. It is self-inherent, there is no need for it. Control is a totally human concept from the point of view of lacking, a mind concept, not a concept of the divine.

Investigate your true wishes using your mind and push it to the limit. Once you find out that it is not the control that you want most, but happiness, you're on solid ground for the rest of the investigation.

Happiness is the key element that we all look for. You can say that money, relationships, or power is what you really want. Can these things bring you true happiness if you are still unable to love and forgive yourself? Without letting go of judgment? Holding strong, self-righteous claims?

Love yourself truly, dearly, and intimately. Forgive yourself, be proud of who you are, and celebrate your individuality, and finally—let go and enjoy the experience.

Fourth key: Freedom from concepts

At the very core of your being lies the most certain fact you know about yourself: the awareness of your own experience, and nothing beyond that, simply the knowledge that you know.

Your understanding of the world and everything you will ever know stems from the vantage point of your experience, a truth shared by everyone else on planet Earth.

Begin your journey of self-discovery by diving deep into the knowing of yourself, viewing the world from the perspective of your experience. Does the world lie outside your skin, or is it within you?

Liberate yourself from the shackles of conditioned concepts of reality, contributed by family, school, friends, and society. Have you ever questioned and pondered over them long enough? After all, these questions are the most significant and mysterious ones in your life.

Could it be that you've missed the point all along?

One day, you opened your eyes to the experience of being alive. Isn't that fact alone astonishing? How did you feel before you came into existence? How did you— the vast, complex, and beautiful being that you are, simply appear out of nowhere? Out of mere cosmic chance?

Certainly, some may offer their explanations, but those people are merely living from someone else's point of view. Do you truly wish to abide by concepts rooted in other people's beliefs or experiences, rather than your own?

To unveil the mysteries about your identity, and the meaning of the big questions we investigate in this book, you must turn inward. Derive your answers from your self-evident experience. Be doubtful in your approach, and fearlessly think it through. Free yourself from concepts entirely, leaving no room for hesitation.

Evaluate each theory, theology, or philosophy, examining them from the perspective of your own experience. Put them into practice and witness their impact firsthand.

Does any of it resonate within you? Does it bring you true satisfaction? Continue your investigation until you find the answers that satisfy your innermost being. The journey may be long, but the rewards are worth the effort. They are the void you are trying to fill.

Fifth key: Anchoring

The idea that enlightenment or the discovery of one's true self can be attained through a specific practice, particularly by attempting to eliminate one's ego, can ironically become the ultimate expression of ego.

Your imaginary self, the one that is constantly bouncing and riding the crazy waves of the mind, can often present itself to be your true nature, your intuitive heart.

So, you might say, how do I know which one is which?

Unfortunately, I don't know of any specific method, nor have I heard any compelling suggestions. What I've discovered is that it's a gradual process of reconnecting and reestablishing self-awareness.

The practice that I found to be effective was letting mistakes happen and anchoring.

When I made the decision to trust my own true nature and listen to my heart, I did so by opening myself up to the possibility that I might make mistakes.

In the long run, these mistakes would be the learning curve for the intimate knowledge of my true nature in what I really want and what makes me happy.

I listen to what my intuitive heart says. Yes, mistakes happen. In fact, they must happen in order to improve your flow, your craft in life. So, treat it as an art form. For instance, when I play the guitar, I make many mistakes, but are they mistakes? Or are they my lessons? If I made no mistakes, how would I improve in the art of playing music?

When a mistake happens, ask yourself what the benefits of the mistake are and learn from them. It might be a blessing in disguise.

And as you get closer to your mind-heart, the answers to decisions will naturally present themselves. Without requiring effort in making a choice, you will feel it, and trust it to be so without the need for approval from others, or even from your own thoughts.

Understand that you will make mistakes regardless, but it is far better to trust the one thing you know for sure and stick to it, rather than using different strategies all the time. You are bound to fail if you do.

The concept of anchoring entered my life after the challenging experience I went through during my mushroom trip. When I snapped out of my state of madness, I realized that while I was battling demons, suffering, and agonizing, the underlying reality was the room. I was just in the room and none of the rest was real. It was all manifested by thought and perception. The room was the only reality, I was the only reality.

My anchoring is, "I am just in my room, that's all."

So, as I catch a ride on the crazy train of thought, I go back to the room analogy to help me snap out of it. Then I go back to the beautiful reality that underlines it all.

Look for your anchor, find it and use it in your journey.

Sixth key: Not forcing

Be like a shaman in your approach to life, look at everything with curiosity. Observe nature, listen to your intuitive heart, the sounds and vibrations of the air, the crashing waves of the ocean, and the interplay of your senses with it all. Everything holds meaning.

Although some will claim the intuitive heart is only a belief and no more, I would ask them, "What is the nature of other thoughts in your mind you validate over your counterintuition? Do they come with a certificate of truth? Do you trust "truth" due to a social consensus? If so, how many times has the consensus changed in history?"

It's just the inner knowledge of your true nature that will call you to act.

Think of the phenomenon of electricity.

When you connect your electric teapot to electricity, it makes the water boil. The same electricity gives life to your mobile phone. Two completely different devices, with different levels of sophistication and elegance, but nevertheless powered by the same phenomenon we call electricity.

Electricity has no form before it is manifested into form. It takes form through objects, through certain arrangements and conditions, and then expresses itself through them.

Your ego, or separate self, is the teapot, the phone, and you are the electricity. The formless, shapeless energy that manifests the universe. Your individuality is a condition and a form through which the electricity of life—the great "Tau" as the Chinese call it—operates.

You, the electricity, take form in certain conditions and celebrate your individuality by expressing yourself.

Whether bound or unbound to the illusory self, electricity will continue to operate. It's up to you to recognize your nature and potential, enabling you to express your individuality through the electricity that defines you—the ultimate reality veiled by illusion.

When you let the electricity flow within you, it flows without resistance, like a mirror that does not resist any reflection. When you resist it, it grates against you and you can feel it in every aspect of your life.

Express yourself, don't let fear rattle your bones. Remember that you are always one with the works of the cosmos. Only with trust and experience can you see it for yourself. One that stands in the corner at a party can't understand the enjoyment of the dance.

Words, like other symbols, can only go as far as any good philosopher can put them. True recognition of the flow is not to be explained by words alone, not to be totally grasped by the mind, nor should it be so. Otherwise, it would lose its own magic of formlessness. Imagine explaining a musical piece in words. No matter how deep you go, how articulate you are, it will be a whole different experience when it is actually heard.

Fish swim to the rhythm of the sea and birds fly according to the rhythm of the air without them needing to think it through.

Don't use force to look for your own rhythm, and don't fake your spontaneity or your individuality. The result will only be an illusion of the mind and will make you appear fake, without any authenticity. Condition yourself to be in the flow, and the rhythm of individuality will arise from within. In ancient Chinese philosophy, this way of living is known as "Wu Wei", meaning, "without forcing."

When you try and force your way in, you might get through, but it will only end up being a revolving door back to the illusion.

The art of not forcing comes from the recognition of your true nature. You are the electricity, not the teapot, not the mobile phone. Thus, you recognize that by letting go you will achieve whatever is needed to be achieved.

Align with your intuition, your heart-mind, and let your own invisible powers of electricity guide you through this journey of life, of human experience.

One makes a fool of oneself by overpowering a world that will no longer be available to him when he dies. The electricity of life is far greater and superior to thought and perception. It is superior to everything as it is the basic underlying reality of existence.

Live a joyful life by recognizing your true nature and letting the electricity express your unique individuality with total trust and free flow.

Without fear, shame, or any psychological trap, this is the way of liberation from the tyranny of the mind and the separation between "you" and "other."

Teachers might get caught in their own methods, but a student has no such problems. Be a student of life and enjoy the exploration. This kind of path will open up the opportunity to participate in the human game with the curiosity of a first-time explorer, and allow space to your individual authenticity. This mindful approach will empower you to realize the beauty and wonder that surrounds you, making each day special, unique, and meaningful.

Keep your heart and mind open as if life starts for you today, right here, right now. Enjoy the fruits of this journey and also appreciate its traps, pitfalls, and letdowns. Because, when the time comes, you will have to let it all go; whatever it may be. As I mentioned at the beginning of this book—this isn't the kind of book that instructs you to perform a unique formula, nor does it follow a certain doctrine. Even when you find yourself, you may still lose sight of it from time to time – that's the nature of the human experience.

The quest for self-realization, the understanding of one's being, is not an endgame; it's merely a part of the game, just as valid as being completely immersed in the illusion. Being aware of this will keep you fulfilled and engaged in truly living, regardless of the direction your experience may take. Making mistakes is okay, feeling mixed up and confused is okay, and embracing profound understanding is also okay. Shifting between these states will allow you to uncover the gems in each, as there are always gems to be found in any experience.

Enjoy the process as you would enjoy a musical concert, a movie, a dream, or a game. The process itself holds the meaning, not the endgame, for many of us understand that the game itself is the pinnacle of the activity, and that an end is simply another chance for a new beginning, as they are intertwined. If you can, extend kindness to others, as they are also you in different forms, shaping the reality of this world, each with their own unique, special, and valuable essence.

Dive into your feelings, whether they're positive or negative, but especially the challenging ones, because the positive feelings often need no explanation or exploration.

Appreciate yourself for who you are, and embrace the form you've taken in this world. Love it, nurture it, and express yourself through it. This is the other side of fear, judgment, and self-destruction.

This is the key to happiness.

Made in the USA
Monee, IL
25 October 2023